What on Earth?
An Ecology Reader

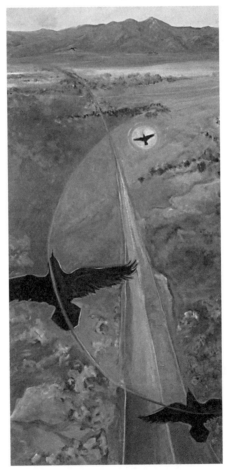

Perfection Learning

EDITORIAL DIRECTOR	Julie A. Schumacher
SENIOR EDITOR	Terry Ofner
EDITOR	Rebecca Christian
PERMISSIONS	Laura Pieper
REVIEWERS	Mary Gershon
	Lynne Albright
	Ann Tharnish

DESIGN AND PHOTO RESEARCH

Jan Michalson
Lisa Lorimor

COVER ART RIDING THE WIND (detail) 1997 Carey Moore
Oil, 48" x 24". Printed with permission of the artist, 2000.

ACKNOWLEDGMENTS

"All Revved Up About an Even Bigger Vehicle" by Dave Barry. Reprinted by permission of The Miami Herald.

"And They Lived Happily Ever After for a While" from *Fast and Slow*. Copyright © 1975 by John Ciardi. Reprinted by permission of Houghton Mifflin Co. All rights reserved.

"Animals, Vegetables and Minerals" by Jessica Szymczyk. From *Newsweek*, August 14, 1995. All rights reserved. Reprinted by permission.

"Baptisms" by Joseph Bruchac. © Joseph Bruchac 1999.

"Battle for the Rain Forest" by Joe Kane. From *Scholastic Update*, February 8, 1999 issue. Copyright © 1999 by Scholastic Inc. Reprinted by permission of Scholastic Inc.

"David Meets Goliath at City Hall" by Andrew Holleman. Reprinted by permission of the author. Originally printed in *Mother Earth News*, March–April 1990.

"Duck Hunting" by Gary Paulsen. From *Father Water, Mother Woods* by Gary Paulsen Ill. Ruth Wright Paulsen, copyright text 1994 by Gary Paulsen. Illustrations 1994 by Ruth Wright Paulsen. Used by permission of Dell Publishing, a division of Random House, Inc.

"A Fable for Tomorrow" from *Silent Spring* by Rachel Carson. Copyright © 1962 by Rachel L. Carson. Copyright © renewed 1990 by Roger Christie. Reprinted by permission of Houghton Mifflin Company. All rights reserved.

"The Face of a Spider" by David Quammen. Reprinted by permission of David Quammen. All rights reserved. Copyright © 1987 by David Quammen.

"For Richard Chase" by Jim Wayne Miller. Reprinted by permission of Mary Ellen Miller.

CONTINUED ON PAGE 151

HOW DO WE PROTECT OUR PLANET?

The question above is the *essential question* that you will consider as you read this book. The literature, activities, and organization of the book will lead you to think critically about this question and to develop a deeper understanding of ecology.

To help you shape your answer to the broad essential question, you will read and respond to four sections, or clusters. Each cluster addresses a specific question and thinking skill.

CLUSTER ONE What is our relationship with nature? **EVALUATE**

CLUSTER TWO What happens when humanity and nature collide? **ANALYZE**

CLUSTER THREE How can we live in harmony with nature? **PROBLEM SOLVE**

CLUSTER FOUR Thinking on your own **SYNTHESIZE**

Notice that the final cluster asks you to think independently about your answer to the essential question—*How do we protect our planet?*

ONLY A LITTLE PLANET

LAWRENCE COLLINS

The planet you're standing on
looking out at the stars
is the earth, the third planet from the sun

and the mildest
and softest
of the nine....

If you can stop, and let yourself look,
let your eyes do what they do best,
stop
and let yourself see and see
that everything is doing things
to you
as you do things to everything.

Then you know
that although it is only a little planet
it is hugely beautiful
and surely the finest place in the world
to be.

So watch it, look at it
see what it's like
to walk around on it.
It's small but it's beautiful
It's small but it's fine
like a rainbow,

like a bubble.

Table of Contents

Butterfly or Asteroid?

There once was a butterfly that lived in the jungles of Brazil. One day, a single beat of its wings set a remarkable series of events in motion. In a mere two weeks, a tornado in Texas was the result.

This little story is a favorite of scientists working in a field called "chaos theory." They say it demonstrates a fascinating and alarming fact—that even very small actions can have huge consequences.

It could happen this way: the mere flutter of the butterfly's wings produces a puff of air. The puff might gather into a breeze, the breeze might escalate into a wind, the wind might whip itself into a much more dramatic weather pattern, until a tornado is created.

There is another story scientists who study the history of life on earth like to tell. They believe that a giant asteroid struck the earth about 65 million years ago, its force creating a crater 120 miles across and triggering fires, earthquakes, volcanoes, and mass extinction. Some say it plunged the planet into darkness and may even have caused the disappearance of the dinosaurs.

The asteroid story brings up the point that while we humans can and do harm our environment, natural disasters can be just as devastating, if not more so. In fact, if all the nuclear weapons in today's world were detonated at once, their explosion would be more than a thousand times smaller than this asteroid's impact!

Some environmentalists believe we are living through another great mass extinction right now. It began thousands of years ago, when human beings first appeared on the earth. Some say it is accelerating to the point where several species are vanishing every hour. Environmental photographer Mark Carwardine cautions, "No one knows how close to the limit we are getting. The darker it gets, the faster we're driving."

An Inca proverb observes, "The frog does not drink up the pond in which it lives." Yet sometimes we humans befoul our own pond through pollution, overconsumption of natural resources, and runaway population growth.

So are we like a giant asteroid?

No.

For one thing, an asteroid could destroy our planet and all life on it. Despite some alarmist claims, we humans cannot do this. As biologist Lynn Margulis wrote, "We cannot put an end to nature. We can only pose a threat to ourselves."

More importantly, an asteroid cannot choose its course. We can choose ours. As you will see in the pages that follow, every day more people are taking action to protect our planet and the astonishing creatures with which we share it. The reason so many people devote their lives to protecting animals, Carwardine says, is simple: "The world would be a poorer, darker, lonelier place without them."

Fortunately, we are more like the Brazilian butterfly than an asteroid. Like the butterfly, even our smallest actions can have great consequences. But also like the butterfly, we are a small part of a big picture. Nature is tough, and we are fragile.

To think of ourselves as a butterfly is humbling. And humility may be just what our species needs to make our planet thrive.

Thinking Naturally

Nature can't take any more animals as successful as man.

Farley Mowat, naturalist

We reached the old wolf in time to watch a fierce green fire dying in her eyes. I realized then, and have known ever since, that there was something new to me in those eyes—something known only to her and to the mountain. I was young then, and full of trigger-itch; I thought that because fewer wolves meant more deer, that no wolves would mean hunters' paradise. But after seeing the green fire die, I sensed that neither the wolf nor the mountain agreed with such a view.

Aldo Leopold, naturalist

My childhood dream was...to watch free, wild animals living their own undisturbed lives. I wanted to learn things that no one else knew, uncover secrets through patient observation. I wanted to come as close to talking to the animals as I could.

Jane Goodall, a primatologist who conducts research with chimpanznzees

When I climbed this tree I gave my word to her, to the forest and to all the people that my feet would not touch the ground until I had done everything in my power to make the world aware of this problem and to stop the destruction.

Julia Butterfly Hill, an environmental activist who prevented a California redwood from being felled through a dramatic protest—she lived in its top branches for two years.

We humans take our Earth for granted and never hesitate to exploit it and its other inhabitants to gratify our immediate wants. We have to understand that we are part of nature, not outside of it. What we do to the Earth, we do to ourselves.

Petra K. Kelly, co-founder of the German Green Party

Wildlife is something which man cannot construct. Once it is gone, it is gone forever. Man can rebuild a pyramid, but he can't rebuild ecology, or a giraffe.

Joy Adamson, author of Born Free *and a pioneer in protecting endangered animals, particularly lions*

The most important thing about Spaceship Earth: an instruction book didn't come with it.

R. Buckminster Fuller, inventor and philosopher

Thousands of tired, nerve-shaken, over-civilized people are beginning to find out that going to the mountains is going home; that wildness is a necessity; and that mountain parks and reservations are useful not only as fountains of timber and irrigating rivers, but as fountains of life.

John Muir, Father of American national parks

CONCEPT VOCABULARY

You will find the following terms and definitions useful as you read and discuss the selections in this book.

biodiversity the degree of variety in an environment measured by the number of different species of plants and animals

biosphere living things together with their environment

carcinogen a substance that causes cancer

dominion absolute ownership; supreme authority

ecosystem an interconnnected community of living things, such as the ecosystem of the rain forest or prairie

endangered species a species, or type, of plant or animal in danger of becoming extinct

energy efficiency how well something works compared to how much it costs, either in dollars or other resources such as fuel or human labor

extinct no longer existing

global warming a theory that the overall temperature of the earth is rising due to the greenhouse effect

green or **greeny** an environmentalist, especially one in an activist group such as Greenpeace

greenhouse effect a theory that the earth is warming due to gasses in the upper atmosphere, such as carbon dioxide and methane, that trap the heat of the sun

human-induced caused by people

ozone layer the layer of the atmosphere that blocks ultraviolet radiation from the sun; some environmentalists believe that the ozone layer is disappearing, causing global warming

naturalist a person who studies natural history; particularly a biologist who spends much working time in nature

pristine unspoiled

steward one who supervises, protects, or manages carefully and responsibly

tree-hugger a negative term for an extreme environmentalist

toxic poisonous

CLUSTER ONE

What Is Our Relationship with Nature?
Thinking Skill EVALUATING

The Growin' of Paul Bunyan

William J. Brooke

This is a story about how Paul Bunyan met up with Johnny Appleseed an' what come about because o' that meetin'. But it all got started because o' the problems Paul had with his boots one mornin'.

The hardest thing for ole Paul about gettin' started in the mornin' was puttin' on his boots. It wasn't so much the lacin' up that got him down (although when your bootlaces are exactly 8,621 feet an' four an' three-quarters inches long, an' each one has to be special ordered from the Suwanee Steamship Cable Company in New York City, an' if because you're strong as ole Paul you tend to snap about two laces a week as a rule, then just tyin' your boots can be a bit of an irritation, too).

No, the hardest part o' puttin' on his boots was makin' sure he was the only one in 'em. Because, you see, they was so big an' warm that all the critters liked to homestead in 'em. So he'd have to shake 'em for nine or ten minutes just to get out the ordinary rattlesnakes an' polecats. Then he'd reach in an' feel around real careful for mountain lions an' wolf packs an' the occasional caribou migration. Fin'ly he'd wave his hand around real good to see if any hawks or eagles was huntin' game down around the instep. Then he could start the chore o' lacin'.

But ever' now an' then, no matter how careful he was, he'd miss a critter or two an' then he'd just have to put up with it. 'Cause once he had those laces all done up, it just wasn't worth the trouble to untie 'em all again.

So on this partic'lar day ole Paul is out o' sorts because of a moose that's got stuck down betwixt his toes. Paul's appetite is so spoiled he can't get down more than three hunnert pancakes an' about two an' a half hogs worth o' bacon afore he grabs up his ax an' takes off to soothe his ragged nerves in his usual way, by shavin' a forest or two.

Well, the more his toes itch, the faster he chops; an' the faster he chops, the more his toes itch. Fin'ly he can't stand it no more, so he sets down on a medium-size mountain an' undoes all 8,621 feet, four an' three-quarters inches o' his right bootlace an' takes it off an' shakes it out for twenty minutes afore he remembers it was his left foot that was itchin'. So he gives a big sigh an' starts in on the other boot.

Fin'ly both boots is off, an' a slightly bruised moose is shakin' his head an' blinkin' his eyes an' staggerin' off betwixt the stumps. An' Paul has his first chance to take a deep breath an' have a look round. An' he's surprised, 'cause he can't see any trees anywheres, only stumps. So he gets up on a stump an' looks around, an' he still can't see any standin' timber. He'd been so wrought up, he'd cleared all the way to the southern edge o' the woods without noticin'.

Now this annoys Paul, 'cause he's too far from camp to get back for lunch, an' nothin' upsets him like missin' grub. An' when he's upset, the only thing to soothe him is choppin' trees, an' all the trees is down, so that annoys him even worse.

There he sits, feelin' worse by the minute, with his stomach growlin' like a thunderstorm brewin' in the distance. An' then he notices somethin' way off at the horizon, out in the middle o' them dusty brown plains. All of a sudden there's somethin' green. As he watches, that green starts to spread in a line right across the middle of all that brown.

Now the only thing I ever heard tell of that was bigger than ole Paul hisself was ole Paul's curiosity. It was even bigger than his appetite. So, quick as he can get his boots on, he's off to see what's happenin'. What he sees makes him stop dead in his tracks. 'Cause it's trees, apple trees growin' where nothin' but dirt ever growed before. A whole line of apple trees stretchin' in both directions as far as you can see.

It makes him feel so good he just has to take up his ax an' start choppin'. An' the more he chops, the better he feels. An' as he marches westward through all the flyin' splinters an' leaves an' applesauce, he sees that the trees is gettin' shorter until they're just saplin's, then green shoots, then just bare earth.

Paul stops short then an' leans on his ax handle to study the funny little man who turns around an' looks up at him. He's barefoot an' wears a gunnysack for clothes, with a metal pot on his head for a hat. He looks up at Paul for a second, then reaches in a big bulgy bag hangin' at his side an' takes out somethin' teeny-tiny, which he sticks in the ground. He gathers the dusty brown dirt around it an' pats it down. He stands up, an' out of a canvas water bag he pours a little bit o' water on the spot. Then he just stands an' watches.

For a few seconds nothin' happens; then the tiniest, littlest point o' green pokes out o' the dust an' sort o' twists around like it's lookin' for somethin'. All at once, it just stretches itself toward the sky an' pulls a saplin' up after it. An' it begins to branch an' to fill out, an' its smooth green skin turns rough an' dark an' oozes sap. The branches creak an' groan an' stretch like a sleeper just wakin' up. Buds leaf out an' turn their damp green faces to the sun. An' the apples change from green to red an' swell like balloons full to bustin' with sweet cider.

The funny little man looks up an' smiles an' says, "My name's John Chapman, but folks call me Johnny Appleseed."

"Pleased to meet you," says Paul.

The little man points at his tree. "Mighty pretty sight, don't you think?"

"Sure is," says Paul, an' with a quick-as-a-wink flick o' his ax, he lays the tree out full length on the ground. "My name's Paul Bunyan."

The little man lifts his tin pot an' wipes his bald head while he stares at the tree lyin' there in the dirt. Then he squints up at Paul an' kneels down an' puts another seed in the ground. Paul smiles down at him while the tree grows up, then lays it out by the first. The little man pops three seeds into the ground fast as can be. Paul lets 'em come up, then lops all three with one easy stroke, backhand.

"You sure make 'em come up fast," says Paul, admirin'-like.

"It's a sort o' gift I was born with," says Johnny Appleseed. He looks at the five trees lyin' together. "You sure make 'em come down fast."

"It's a talent," says Paul, real humble. "I have to practice a lot."

They stand quiet awhile, with Paul leanin' easy on his ax an' Johnny lookin' back along the line o' fallen trees to the horizon. He lifts his tin pot again an' rubs even harder at his head. Then he looks up at Paul an' says, "It seems like we got somethin' of a philosophical difference here."

Paul considers that. "We both like trees," he says, real friendly.

"Yep," Johnny nods, "but I like 'em vertical an' you like 'em horizontal."

Paul agrees but says he don't mind a man who holds a differin' opinion from his own, 'cause that's what makes America great. Johnny says, "Course you don't mind, 'cause when my opinion has finished dif- ferin' an' the dust settles, the trees is in the position you prefer. Anybody likes a fight that he always wins."

Paul allows he's sorry that Johnny's upset. "But loggin's what I do, an' a man's gotta do what he does. Besides, without my choppin' lumber, you couldn't build houses or stoke fires or pick your teeth."

"I don't live in a house, an' I don't build fires, an' when I want to clean my teeth, I just eat an apple. Tell me, when all the trees are gone, what'll you cut down then?"

Paul laughs. "Why, there'll always be trees. Are you crazy or somethin'?"

"Yep," says Johnny, "crazy to be wastin' time an' lung power on you. I got to be off. I'm headin' for the Pacific Ocean, an' I got a lot o' work to do on the way. So why don't you head north an' I'll head west, an' our paths won't cross till they meet somewheres in China."

Paul feels a little hurt at this, but he starts off north, then stops to watch as Johnny takes off at a run, tossin' the seed out in front o' him, pressin' it down into the ground with his bare toes, an' tricklin' a little water behind, all without breakin' stride. In a minute he's vanished at the head o' his long line of apple trees.

▲   ▲   ▲

Now Paul has figured that Johnny hadn't really meant to offend him, but it was more in the nature of a challenge. An' Paul loves any kind of a challenge. So he sets down an' waits three days, figurin' he should give a fair head start to Johnny, who's a couple hunnert feet shorter'n he is. Then at dawn on the fourth day, he stands up an' stretches an' holds his ax out level a foot above the ground. When he starts to run, the trees drop down in a row as neat as the crossties on a railroad line. In fact, when it came time to build the transcontinental railroad, they just laid the iron rails down on that long line o' apple trees an' saved theirselves many thousands o' dollars.

Anyways, Paul runs for two days an' two nights, an' when the sun's settin' on the third day, he sees water up ahead. There's Johnny Appleseed plantin' a last tree, then sittin' on a high, bare bluff lookin' out over the Pacific Ocean. Paul finishes the last o' the trees an' swings the ax over his head with a whoop an' brings it down on the dirt, buryin' its head in the soil an' accident'ly creatin' the San Andreas fault. He mops his brow an' sits down beside Johnny, with his feet danglin' way down into the ocean.

Starin' out at the orange sun, Johnny asks, "Are they all gone?" Paul looks back over his shoulder an' allows as how they are. Paul waits for Johnny to say somethin' else, but he just keeps starin', so Paul says, "It took you six days to plant 'em an' it took me only three days to chop 'em

down. Pretty good, huh?"

Johnny looks up an' smiles sadly. "It's always easier to chop somethin' down than to make it grow." Then he goes back to starin'.

Now that rankles Paul. When he beats somebody fair an' square, he expects that someone to admit it like a man. "What's so hard about growin' a tree anyway?" he grumps. "You just stick it in the ground, an' the seed does all the work."

Johnny reaches way down in the bottom o' his bag an' holds out a seed. "It's the last one," he says. "All the rest o' my dreams is so much kindlin' wood, so why don't you take this an' see if it's so easy to make it grow."

Paul hems an' haws, but he sees as how he has to make good on his word. So he takes the little bitty seed an' pushes it down in the ground with the tip o' one fingernail. He pats the soil around it real nice, like he seen Johnny do. Then he sits down to wait as the sun sets.

"I'm not as fast as you at this," Paul says, "but you've had more practice. An' I'm sure my tree will be just as good as any o' yours."

"Not if it dies o' thirst," says Johnny's voice out o' the dark.

Paul hasn't thought about that. So when the moon comes up, he heads back to a stream he passed about two hunnert miles back. But he don't have nothin' to carry water in, so he scoops up a double handful an' runs as fast as he can, with the water slippin' betwixt his fingers. When he gets back, he's got about two drops left.

"Guess I'll have to get more water," he says, a mite winded.

"Don't matter," says Johnny's voice, "if the rabbits get the seed."

An' there in the moonlight, Paul sees all the little cottontails hoppin' around an' scratchin' at the ground. Not wishin' to hurt any of 'em, he picks 'em up, one at a time, an' moves 'em away, but they keep hoppin' back. So, seein' as how he still needs water, he grabs 'em all up an' runs back to the stream, sets the rabbits down, grabs up the water, runs back, flicks two more drops on the spot, pushes away the new batch o' rabbits movin' in, an' tries to catch his breath.

"Just a little more water an' a few less rabbits an' it'll be fine," Paul says between gasps.

Out o' the dark comes Johnny's voice. "Don't matter, if the frost gets it."

Paul feels the cold ground, an' he feels the moisture freezin' on his hands. So he gets down on his knees, an' he folds his hands around that little spot o' dirt an', gentle as he can, breathes his warm breath onto that tiny little seed. Time passes, and the rabbits gather round to enjoy the warmth an' scratch their soft little backs up against those big callused hands. As the night wears on, Paul falls into a sleep, but his hands never stop cuppin' that little bit o' life.

Sometime long after moonset, the voice o' Johnny Appleseed comes driftin' soft out o' the dark an' says, "Nothin's enough if you don't care enough."

Paul wakes up with the sun. He sets up an' stretches, an' for a minute he can't remember where he is. Then he looks down, an' he gives a whoop. 'Cause he sees a little tiny bit o' green pokin' up through the grains o' dirt. "Hey, Johnny," he yells, "look at this!" But Johnny Appleseed is gone, slipped away in the night. Paul is upset for a minute, then realizes he don't need to brag to anybody, that that little slip o' green is all the happiness he needs right now.

As the sun rises, he fetches more water an' shoos away the crows an' shields that shoot from the heat o' the sun. It grows taller an' straighter an' puts out buds an' unfurls its leaves. Paul carries in all the animals from the surroundin' countryside, coyotes an' sidewinders[1] an' Gila monsters,[2] an' sets 'em down in a circle to admire his tree growin' tall an' sturdy an' green.

▲ ▲ ▲

Then Paul notices somethin'. He gets down on his hands an' knees an' looks close. It's a brown leaf. "That's not too serious," he thinks, an' he shades it from the sun. Then he sees another brown leaf, an' he runs back to get more water. When he gets back, the little saplin' is droopin' an' shrivelin'. He gets down an' breathes on it, but as he watches, the leaves drop off an' the twigs snap. "Help me, somebody," he cries out, "help me!" But there's no answer 'cept the rustlin' o' of the critters as they slink away from him. An' while he looks down at the only thing he ever give birth to, it curls up an' dies.

For a second he just stands there; then he pounds his fists on the ground an' yells, "Johnny! Johnny! Why didn't you tell me how much it could hurt?"

He sets down an' he stares till the sun begins settin'. Then he jumps up an' says, "Only one thing's gonna make me feel better. I'm gonna cut me some timber! Maybe a whole forest if I can find one!" He reaches for his ax.

An' that's when he sees it. It stretches right up to the sky, with great green boughs covered with sweet-smellin' needles an' eagles nestin' in its heights. Johnny must have worked some o' his magic afore he left, 'cause when Paul struck it into the ground, it wasn't nothin' but an ax. But now, in the light o' the settin' sun, it shines like a crimson column crowned in evergreen.

"I'll call it a redwood," says Paul, who knew now he'd never want an ax again as long as there was such a tree.

So he waited for the cones with the seeds to form an' drop, an' he planted them all over the great Northwest an' nurtured them an' watched a great woodland spring up in their shelter. An' he never felled a tree again as long as he lived.

For years he worked, an' there are those who say you can still catch a glimpse o' him behind the highest mountains in the deepest woods. An' they say he's always smilin' when you see him.

'Cause Paul learned hisself somethin': A little man who chops somethin' down is still just a little man, but there's nobody bigger than a man who learns to grow. ❧

---

1 **sidewinders:** desert rattlesnakes that move sideways

2 **Gila monsters:** poisonous desert lizards

Wisdomkeepers
an Interview with Oren Lyons, Onondaga Tribe

HARVEY ARDEN AND STEVE WALL

A stern-faced Oren Lyons, Faithkeeper of the Turtle Clan of the Onondaga Nation and spokesman for the Six Nations Iroquois Confederacy,[1] sits across a wooden table from us in his log cabin on the Onondaga reservation a few miles south of Syracuse,[2] New York. It's night and the harsh light of a single kerosene lantern casts sharp shadows against the walls and beamed ceiling.

"I prefer no electricity," Oren says. "And no phones. That's important!" In one corner, shrouded in shadow, hangs an assemblage of ceremonial masks, faces turned to the wall. "We show their faces only during ceremonies. And we never allow photographs of our ceremonies, so don't even think of asking." He gives us a long, hard look and shakes his head. "Why come to us? We're the toughest nut to crack. You think we turn our Elders[3] over to anyone who walks in the door?" He leans forward, elbows planted on the table. His eyes probe us. "We guard them like pure spring water. So what is it you guys want from the Elders?" Oren asks. "Secrets? Mystery?" We explain that we want only to meet them and hear whatever they care to share with us, that we're not looking for

---

1 **Turtle Clan of the Onondaga Nation; Six Nations Iroquois Confederacy:** a group within a tribe of American Indians; a league of tribes originally of New York, including the Onondaga

2 **Syracuse:** a city in central New York

3 **Elders:** leaders respected for experience and wisdom

secrets. "That's good," Oren says, "because, I can tell you right now, there are no secrets. There's no mystery. There's only common sense."

He gets up, strides over to the cast-iron stove, and warms his hands. Outside, a cold January wind is moaning, pelting the windows with dry icy snow. We sit uneasily, sure he's about to send us packing into that bitter night. Still rubbing his hands, he sits down and faces us. "Common sense . . . ," he says, picking up the echo of his own words. "I'll tell you guys a little bit about common sense. . . ."

THE NATURAL LAW

"What law are you living under? United States government law? That's Man's law. You break Man's law and you pay a fine or go to jail—maybe. That's the way it is with Man's law. You can break it and still get around it. Maybe you won't get punished at all. Happens all the time. People figure they can get away with anything and half the time they do. But they forget there's another law, the Creator's law. We call it Natural Law . . . Natural law prevails everywhere. It supersedes Man's law. If you violate it, you get hit. There's no judge and jury, there's no lawyers or courts, you can't buy or dodge or beg your way out of it. If you violate this Natural law you're going to get hit and get hit hard.

"One of the Natural laws is that you've got to keep things pure. Especially the water. Keeping the water pure is one of the first laws of life. If you destroy the water, you destroy life. That's what I meant about common sense. Anybody can see that. All life on Mother Earth depends on the pure water, yet we spill every kind of dirt and filth and poison into it. That makes no common sense at all. Your legislature can pass a law saying it's OK, but it's not OK. Natural law doesn't care about your Man's law. Natural law's going to hit you. You can't get out of the way. You don't fool around with Natural law and get away with it. If you kill the water, you kill the life that depends on it, your own included. That's Natural law. It's also common sense."

ALL LIFE IS EQUAL

"Another of the Natural laws is that all life is equal. That's our philosophy. You have to respect life—all life, not just your own. The key word is 'respect.' Unless you respect the earth, you destroy it. Unless you respect all life as much as your own life, you become a destroyer, a murderer. Man sometimes thinks he's been elevated to be the controller, the ruler. But he's not. He's only a part of the whole. Man's job is not to exploit but to oversee, to be a steward. Man has responsibility, not power."

THE SEVENTH GENERATION

"In our way of life, in our government, with every decision we make, we always keep in mind the Seventh Generation to come. It's our job to see that the people coming ahead, the generations still unborn, have a world no worse than ours—and hopefully better. When we walk upon Mother Earth we always plant our feet carefully because we know the faces of our future generations are looking up at us from beneath the ground. We never forget them." Oren slips off into the shadows of the cabin and returns with a beaded wampum belt about four inches wide and a foot and a half long.

THE TWO ROW WAMPUM

"This is a replica of the Two Row Wampum, the basis of our sovereignty. It's the Grandfather of all the treaties between our two peoples. We made it with the Dutch in the early 1600s. The two rows of purple beads represent the Red Man and the White Man living side by side in peace and friendship forever. The white background is a river. On that river of life you travel in your boat and we travel in our canoe. Each of us is responsible for our own government and religion and way of life. We don't interfere with each other. The rows are parallel. One row is not bigger. We're equal. We don't call each other 'Father' or 'Son,' we call each other 'Brother.' That's the way it's supposed to be between us 'for as long as the grass grows and water flows and the sun shines.' Those words come from this treaty. We still believe them. We're waiting for the White Man to live up to his side.

"Right now he's hogging the middle of the river and pushing us aside. But we remember how it's supposed to be, how we agreed in the beginning when you were weak and we were strong. White Man seems to have forgotten. But we've got a long memory. And so has the Creator . . . Our ancestors told us that there will come a time in the future when some of our people will put one foot in the canoe and one in the boat. That's a very precarious position to be in. And they foretold a great wind would rise that would tear the canoe and boat away from each other. Then those people who have one foot in the canoe and one foot in the boat are going to fall into this river. And no power this side of the Creation can save them." ◐

For Richard Chase

JIM WAYNE MILLER

Looking like all outdoors
the old tale-teller from the mountains
enters a highschool classroom in California.

He is himself a mountain:
his face has the lay of coves and hollows.
His shoulders heave up like rock-backed ridges,
His eyes sail and hover like hunting hawks.
Shimmering in his mind like mountain springs,
stories trickle off his tongue, fall
fast, then flow.

Riddles tumble down the stream of his speaking,
gold in gravel.
Even his silences glitter
like streaks of mica[1] in gray rock.

From a knapsack of wonders
the old man takes a seashell.
He holds it to a student's ear and asks:
"What do you hear?"

The student thinks the old man
would make a nice poster
for his bedroom wall
which already has stars
painted on the ceiling.
He listens to the shell and says:
"The freeway?"

---

1 **mica:** a glittery material

Is Humanity a Special Threat?

GREGG EASTERBROOK

In March 1989 the tanker *Exxon Valdez*, carelessly piloted, struck Bligh Reef in Prince William Sound,[1] releasing 11 million gallons of crude oil into a place of pristine beauty and perpetual mists that might as well have been named Brigadoon.[2] Sea birds, otter, and other creatures died by the thousands. Reports described the sound as the site of a "tragedy" or "catastrophe." A judge, ordering the ship's captain jailed, compared the harm done to the atomic bombing of Japan. The sound, it was commonly said, would never recover. Never, ever, ever. "Destroyed" quickly became the official verb for what had happened to the vast Alaskan fiord.

Reaction ought to have been fierce. Both the negligence that caused the spill and arrogance of Exxon executives—the company adopting a position that may be summed up in two words that are not Merry Christmas—represented corporate unaccountability at its most offensive. But was Prince William Sound the site of a catastrophe? A few days after the spill, I wrote an article that included this sentence: "Ten years from now the sound will be so close to its former state that it will be impossible to determine where the spill occurred without resorting to navigation charts." Colleagues urged me not to publish that article, saying I would sacrifice my reputation. After all, the sound was destroyed. Forever and ever.

In 1992, I found myself bobbing through the choppy waters of Prince William Sound aboard the research vessel *Arctic Dream*, crewed by

1 **Prince William Sound:** inlet of the Gulf of Alaska
2 **Brigadoon:** a perfect place remote from time and reality in the musical "Brigadoon"

marine biologists under the sponsorship of the National Oceanographic and Atmospheric Administration, the agency with supervisory responsibility for investigating the spill. Quickly I learned my 1989 prediction had been wrong. It was just three years later, and already the sound was so close to its former state it was impossible to determine where the spill had occurred without resorting to navigation charts. This was true not only of the beaches that had been cleaned but the ones left untouched as well.

Dennis Lees, leader of the team aboard the boat and a researcher who has been studying Prince William Sound since a few days after the spill, used navigation charts to show me where the worst blotches of oil hit. From the deck of the *Arctic Dream*, no sign of oil was apparent anywhere in the sound. Nor could any degradation[3] be seen close to the shore, when the crew disembarked in dinghies.[4] Only by standing on the beach at various points was it possible to observe any residue of petroleum— usually traces below the surface in mussel beds, uncovered by shovel.

Studies clearly show some harm to wildlife in Prince William Sound. Colonies of murries, a bird similar to the penguin, have smaller populations than in 1989, and sightings of killer whales have fallen off in the sound since that year. Herring spawning has declined. But most indicators of life in Prince William Sound are robust. Sea otter, which in the nineteenth century were hunted to near extinction in Alaskan inlets by Russian trawlers,[5] have repopulated the sound with a fervor since being placed under the Marine Mammal Protection Act in 1972. The otter's rate of increase was not interrupted by the spill. Prince William Sound had a record pink salmon catch in 1990, the year after being doused with crude. The salmon run in the sound was rich again in 1991, then declined in 1992 and 1993. Since pinks live just two years, the poor runs involved salmon that did not hatch until after the oil cleared, making some researchers think that the cold spring weather of 1992 and 1993, which reduced the plankton on which salmon feed, caused the drop.

It turned out that Lees's greatest concern about Prince William Sound was not wildlife loss, which he considered bad but a one-time effect; Lees's concern was that the cleanup did more damage than the spill. Under pressure from public opinion, Exxon and the Coast Guard committed themselves to a grand-scale cleanup operation that at its peak placed in the sound the greatest concentration of vessels engaged in a

---

3 **degradation:** decline

4 **dinghies:** small boats usually carried on larger boats or towed behind them

5 **trawlers:** boats used for fishing with nets

single operation since the Normandy landing.[6] Hundreds of ships of all sizes anchored in the fiord, motors spewing exhaust and lubricants. Heavy helicopters thundered overhead; floatplanes and seaplanes darted everywhere. Navy landing craft were run ashore on beaches to act as dormitories for cleanup crews, crushing intertidal ecosystems[7] beneath their bulks. In many ways these mechanized intrusions were of greater magnitude to the sound than one spill from a single vessel, even a spill of great proportions.

6 **Normandy landing:** massive landing of troops at the Normandy Invasion, a major World War II battle

7 **intertidal ecosystems:** interrelated plant and animal life along a seashore

The *Arctic Dream* sailed to some beaches, at a place called Block Island, used by Exxon for the before-and-after pictures that grace its Prince William Sound brochures. The sand there looked as fine as the commercially processed sand found at amusement parks. Individual rocks had been scrubbed with hand brushes and even toothpicks; we found an old, oily toothpick in a ravine. We did not, however, find any animals, plant life, or sign of smaller organisms. "It's clean, and it's dead," Lees noted. In many places Exxon used high-pressure hot water to blast away oil. The hot water killed the microbial life on which the food chain is moored. The beaches that were left alone as experimental controls by and large cleansed themselves through wave action, microbic digestion, and other factors: the traditional defenses that nature has prepared against petroleum. The uncleaned beaches cleaned themselves while staying alive in microbial terms.

Lees, who once was Exxon-funded—the company dismissed his environmental consultancy after he questioned the cleanup—believes "the smartest thing they could have done after the spill is not one single thing." The two billion dollars Exxon spent on the cleanup would have generated more environmental benefits had it been used for energy efficiency, or to buy land to place in preservation status, or in any number of other ways. But because a sense of public panic was created regarding the "destruction" of Prince William Sound, this huge sum of money was expended in an enterprise that probably was unneeded and may have done more harm than good.

Why was there a sense of panic surrounding the *Exxon Valdez* in the first place? One reason is pictures. The spill occurred in March, and winter is the clear season for Prince William Sound. Television and newsmagazine camera crews rapidly obtained spectacular footage of oil fouling the intertidal wilderness. Starting around June, the sound often fogs in and stays that way for months, socked in to the weather condition that pilots call flat—fog so close to the ground that long-range photography is out of the question. Had the spill happened during fog season, it would have been a page-six item. The ecological significance of the spill would have been the same, of course, regardless of whether pictures were available. But the significance of ecological events to the government institutions and news organizations that cross-pollinate each other's pantomime hysteria[8] often is determined by factors unrelated to the ecology, such as the availability of pictures.

---

8 **pantomime hysteria:** false frenzy

Why did so many commentators presume Prince William Sound the victim of an instant doom? Petroleum is a naturally occurring product. It "spills" from the earth's crust continuously via seepage, though more slowly than happened at the sound. Because petroleum regularly enters the biosphere on a natural basis, some organisms long ago adapted to metabolizing it. Conceptually what Exxon did was reposition a naturally occurring pollutant from below Earth's surface to an ocean inlet, a place where wave action, sunlight, biology, and other factors immediately began operating in opposition to the intruder.

Of course the biosphere's self-healing ability does not excuse environmental abuses, any more than the regenerative powers of the human body excuse breaking someone's leg. Yet overall nature shrugged off the *Exxon Valdez* "disaster" as if shooing away a mosquito. Prince William Sound went from destroyed to almost like new in about three years, or in less than a single generation for the local large vertebrate species. This is standard operating procedure for the green fortress.[9] ◐

9 **green fortress:** strong and healthy earth

Nacho Loco

GARY SOTO

One morning Ignacio "Nacho" Carrillo's fifth-grade teacher, Mrs. Wigert, brought the book *Fifty Simple Things Kids Can Do to Save the Earth* in to class. She talked about recycling cans and bottles, repairing leaky faucets, planting trees, doing away with Styrofoam, and snipping six-pack rings so birds wouldn't get their necks caught.

"Earth, after all, is our mother," Mrs. Wigert said, and one of the bad boys in the back rows replied, "Yo momma!"

Mrs. Wigert shushed the boy, a finger to her lips. She scanned the class, asking for quiet. Then she announced, "I'm a vegetarian. Do you know what a vegetarian is?"

"It's when you don't like meat," said Desi, a fat boy whose *chones* could be seen when he ran.

"It's when you just eat grass," Leticia said.

"Not grass, Leticia—noodles," Robert corrected.

Mrs. Wigert smiled at these definitions. She said, "It's when you decide not to eat meat for the welfare of your body and the planet."

"I ain't on welfare!" Robert snickered.

The class laughed, and Mrs. Wigert frowned. She clapped the book closed and said that they would go on to math. As she stood up behind her desk, her stomach rumbled, making her sound very, very hungry.

But Nacho had listened to what she said. He knew what a vegetarian was because his brother, Felipe, had gone to college and come back with ideas that would solve the world's problems. His brother had decided not to buy anything at department stores and dressed in clothes from the

Salvation Army thrift store on Tulare Street.

"You're supposed to be educated," his father grumbled at his oldest son. "*¿Por qué te vistes en garras?* Why are you dressed in rags?"

"*Mi'jo,*[1] what will your *abuelita*[2] think?" his mother pleaded.

His father and mother had worked hard to send their son to college, and now, to their minds, he looked like a bum.

And Felipe was a vegetarian.

Yes, Nacho knew what a vegetarian was, and at that moment, as he opened his math book and licked his pencil preparing to do division, he decided to become one. Mrs. Wigert was right, he thought. We must save the planet in small ways.

Nacho left the classroom a committed vegetarian—or at least determined to become one after he ate his lunch, which was weighed down with a thick bologna sandwich. He liked bologna, especially when his mom also packed corn chips in his lunch. He would open his sandwich and methodically place nine corn chips to form a square, as if he were playing tick-tack-toe. Then he'd put it together, close his eyes, and take a big bite, the corn chips crunching in his ears.

And that's what his mother had packed in a paper bag today: a bologna sandwich and corn chips, along with a box of juice and a plastic bag of carrot sticks. Nacho looked at the carrot sticks and put them aside. Then he went to town on the sandwich.

Nacho ate with his friend, Juan, on a bench outside the cafeteria. Juan was one of the best baseball players at school and he could shoot hoop, fight, and keep up with the smartest girls in a spelling bee. He was everything Nacho was not. Nacho was a dreamer, quick to pick up on the most recent scientific fad. Once he read in the "Grab Bag" section of the newspaper that if you place a dull razor blade under a pyramid structure and point it south, the pyramid's energy will restore the sharpness of the blade. He tried it with his father's old blades and wrapped them up as a Christmas present. Unfortunately, the blades remained dull, and his poor father had ended up with nicks from his throat to his upper lip.

"I'm not eating meat after this," Nacho said. "It's bad for the world."

"What are you talking about?" Juan said. His cheeks were fat with bites from a tuna sandwich.

"I'm a vegetarian."

1 **mi'jo:** Spanish for "my son"

2 **abuelita:** Spanish for "little grandmother"

"A what?"

"A vegetarian. I'm a person who thinks of mankind. I won't eat meat anymore." Nacho bit into his juicy bologna sandwich, savoring the taste, eyes closed.

"But you're eating meat now, ain't you?" Juan asked.

"This is the last time," Nacho said, wiping his mouth on the paper bag. His mother had forgotten to pack him a napkin.

"That's weird," Juan said. "Won't you get sick if you don't eat meat?"

"Mrs. Wigert is a vegetarian," Nacho commented.

"She's already grown," Juan said. "Anyways, I like hamburgers."

Nacho saw in his mind's eye a hamburger wrapped in a greasy wrapper and finger-sized french fries steaming on a white plate. He shook the images off and eyed his carrot sticks. He took one out from the sandwich bag and held it in his lips like a cigarette.

"And I don't smoke either," he said, laughing.

After lunch they played baseball, but their game ended when Juan hit the ball onto the roof of a building. Nacho had batted only once, hitting a feeble grounder back to the pitcher.

After school Nacho and Juan walked home together. Both of them were hungry so they stopped at the corner grocery store. Juan scraped up enough money in the corners of his pockets to buy a Hostess cupcake. Nacho bought a package of beef jerky, using the money he got from recycling aluminum cans on Saturday.

"I thought you were a vegetarian," Juan said as they left the store. He tore off the Hostess cupcake wrapper and threw it absentmindedly on the ground.

Nacho's mouth fell open in shock. He stopped in his tracks and confessed, "I am, but I forgot." He looked at the beef jerky; the little chunks reminded him of scabs. But since he had already paid for the beef jerky, he reasoned that it was worse to throw away food than to eat it. He was sure vegetarians would never throw anything away. They would always eat everything on their plates or, in this case, in their packages.

Juan's cellophane scuttled in a light breeze, and Nacho picked it up.

"I'll trade you then," Juan said.

Nacho bit his lip because at the moment he preferred salt to sugar. Reluctantly he handed over his beef jerky. He took Juan's cupcake and stuffed it in his mouth; its chewy sweetness dissolved in three bites. For the rest of the walk home he had to watch Juan tear off pieces of jerky and chew slowly, the smoky juice dripping from his mouth.

Nacho's mother was in the kitchen when he arrived home. The radio was tuned in to Mexican news—a bus had gone off a cliff in Monterrey.

"Hi, Mom," he greeted her, throwing his books on the kitchen table.

"How was your day, *mi hombrecito*?"[3] she asked. She looked up from whacking a round steak with her favorite black-handled kitchen knife. Nacho looked at the round steak, then at the puddle of blood leaking from the meat, and announced, "Mom, I'm a vegetarian."

"*¿Qué?*"[4] she asked. She turned over the steak and started pounding the other side.

"I'm a vegetarian. I don't eat meat anymore."

His mother stopped pounding the steak and wiped her brow with the back of her hand. "Son, don't tell me you're like Felipe."

"Mom, meat is bad for you."

"Meat is good for you. It'll make you *más fuerte*."[5] She made a muscle in her right upper arm.

"Scientists have done studies, Mom. They say our teeth are supposed to eat only vegetables."

"*Ay, Dios,*[6] where did we go wrong!" she cried, her chopping hand waving the kitchen knife.

"Mom, it's for the welfare of our bodies and mankind."

"*Estás chiflado,*[7] just like your brother," she groaned. "And you didn't even go to college." She pounded the steak furiously and mumbled under her breath that when she had been a girl in Mexico, she'd been lucky to eat meat. At the start of a lecture about the old days in Michoacán, when his mother had been the daughter of a poor florist and weekend harpist who plucked his life away at a restaurant, Nacho tiptoed out of the kitchen. He went to his bedroom, which he shared with his little brother, Isaac.

Isaac was watching TV on a small black-and-white set they'd gotten from an uncle who'd needed ten bucks for gas.

"TV's bad for you," Nacho said.

Isaac took his eyes off the television for a second and said, "So?"

"I'm just saying, it's bad. Go ahead and do what you want. I'm a vegetarian." But the television caught Nacho's attention. There was a Burger King commercial of a guy jamming a double patty into a hungry grin.

3 **mi hombrecito:** Spanish for "my little man"

4 **¿Qué?:** Spanish for "What?"

5 **más fuerte:** Spanish for "very strong"

6 **Ay, Dios:** Spanish for "Oh, God"

7 **Estás chiflado:** Spanish for "You are crazy"

Nacho's mouth began to water.

He went outside and played slapball against the garage door. But each time he missed, or the ball ricocheted away from him, he would run past an old cardboard pizza box that had been left on the redwood table under the patio. Nacho remembered that pizza. His father had been promoted to foreman at Valley Irrigation. He and Nacho's mother had gone out to celebrate with their *compa*[8] and brought back spicy pepperoni pizza for the kids.

Nacho played slapball until his father came home, and then the two of them shot hoop. They played a quick game to twelve, one point per basket. His father was big around the middle but a sweet outside shooter.

"You're just a little *piojo*,[9] but you'll grow," his father said, wiping his face with the sleeve of his work shirt. He sat on the back steps. His chest was heaving, and the lines on his throat glistened with sweat.

"Dad," Nacho said, "I think I might be a vegetarian."

"*¿Qué dices*?"[10] his father asked, his face still.

"Today we had a talk about the world. Mrs. Wigert said eating meat is bad for you."

"So?"

"So, I'm a vegetarian. I don't eat meat anymore."

"*¿Qué hacen a mi familia*?[11] First your brother and now you?" His father got up and turned on the garden hose. He drank long and hard from it. He patted his belly and then agreed, "OK, you be a vegetaran . . ."

"*Vegetarian*," Nacho said.

"Yes, but you'll be such a *flaco*[12] we won't know where you are," he said playfully. "Not like this." He smacked his belly and laughed.

His father went inside, leaving Nacho on the back steps staring at the empty pizza box. When he finally went inside, his older brother, Felipe, was in the kitchen, lowering a piece of *carne asada*—marinated round steak—into his mouth.

"Hey, Felipe," Nacho said, his stomach suddenly grumbling from emptiness.

"Hey, you little Nacho-head," Felipe said to his brother. "Give me five."

---

8   **compa:** Spanish for "group of friends"

9   **piojo:** Spanish for "louse"

10   **¿Qué dices?:** Spanish for "what did you say?"

11   **¿Qué hacen a mi familia?:** Spanish for "What is happening to my family?"

12   **flaco:** Spanish for "skinny person"

They slapped each other's hands. Then Nacho said, "I thought you were a vegetarian."

"Not anymore. My girlfriend left me."

"What?"

"Yeah, she moved on to greener pastures. A lawyer. I guess she doesn't like accountants."

"You mean you were a vegetarian because of your girlfriend?" Nacho was shocked. He turned on the faucet in the kitchen and washed his hands.

"Sort of. But I have a new girlfriend. She likes good food and bad movies."

"But I thought you had principles!"

"I do. But I got a new girlfriend."

Nacho felt cheated. He wanted to tell Felipe that he had become a vegetarian, but he kept quiet.

From the dining room their father called, "*Hombres,*[13] let's eat."

"Chow time," Felipe said.

Felipe sat down, a napkin crushed in one hand and a fork shining in the other. After a prayer of thanks, during which he kept his eyes open looking at the meat, Felipe dove into the *carne asada*. He ate like a barbarian, ripping a tortilla and pinching up smudges of *frijoles*.[14]

"See, if you were living at home you would be eating good," his mother said as she passed him another tortilla from the basket.

"*Claro,*"[15] he said.

Nacho sat in front of his plate of rice and beans. He took a forkful of beans, eyeing his brother's plate, which was loaded with steaming meat. He looked at his little brother's face, his mother's face, and his father's dark and stubbled face: they were all enjoying meat. They were barbarian meat-eaters.

Later Nacho helped do the dishes. He rinsed while his mother washed, and he kept turning around and looking at the stove; the pan of meat still rested on one of the burners. His mouth watered.

After the dishes were done, the family sat and watched a sitcom on television. Nacho didn't care about the program, except when one of the actors lifted a fork or wiped his mouth on a cloth napkin. But he zeroed

---

13 **Hombres:** Spanish for "men"

14 **frijoles:** Spanish for "beans"

15 **Claro:** Spanish for "clear;" here it means "true" or "right"

in on the Denny's commercial and its parade of fried chicken, burgers, club sandwiches, bacon and eggs, and milk shakes. While they watched television, Nacho's father told his son Felipe that he was proud of him.

"You went all the way," he said. "In a few years it will be Nacho's turn. Already he has big ideas, like being a . . . *cómo*?"[16]

"A vegetarian," Nacho's mother said. She had changed the channel to *las noticias*, the evening news.

"Yes, a human who doesn't eat meat," his father said. "How he will grow, *no sé*."[17]

"That's cool," Felipe said to Nacho. "Start young. What grade are you in?"

"Fifth," Nacho said, staring at a commercial for Pioneer Chicken.

"Yeah, go to State. I'll tell you about financial aid."

"Yes, ask about money. This ol' burro won't last," his father said, pointing to himself and braying like a donkey. "Ask your teacher *también*."[18]

Nacho heard some of their chatter, but his eyes were locked on the screen. A bucket of chicken was being devoured by a family of five, just like their family. Nacho's mouth flooded with the waters of hunger, and he had to leave the living room to eat a cracker.

Nacho went to bed hungry but determined not to ruin the planet. He lay awake, thinking about food, and when he closed his eyes, he saw a floating chicken drumstick.

But as he moved toward sleep he told himself that he should get serious. The next day he was going to ask Mrs. Wigert about college—financial aid, majors, and easy courses. And in privacy, away from Juan and the others, he was going to ask point-blank: how can you live without meat? ∾

---

16 **¿como?**: Spanish for "what?"
17 **no sé**: Spanish for "I don't know"
18 **también**: Spanish for "also"

Baptisms

JOSEPH BRUCHAC

Believing that people
were or became
what they were named,
they rose with the Sun,
called themselves Eagle,
Fox, Otter, Hawk, Wolf,
Bear and Deer.

Then new ones came,
those who named
themselves for forgotten memories,
great-grandfathers seeking
hard dominion over rock and stream,
ownership of forest and plain,
with names of Farmer, Smith and Weaver,
Joiner, Carpenter, Stoner, Wright.

Then they gave
the first people new names,
Government men and preachers smiled
as they christened Washingtons,
Wilsons, Garcias, Smiths—
and waited for them to change.

Yet even today,
when the newest names,
Citizen Band, Breeder Reactor,
Missile Range, Strip Mine and Pipe Line
have begun to move in,
residing where Bark Lodge, Wigwam
and Tipi, Wickiup and Hogan[1] stood,
things have not ended as they should.

Somewhere, it is whispered,
at some ragged edge
of the unfinished land
the Sun is rising, breathing again
names which we have not yet heard,
names about to be spoken.

---

1 **bark lodge, wigwam, tipi, wickiup and hogan:** Native American dwellings

Responding to Cluster One

What Is Our Relationship with Nature?

Thinking Skill EVALUATING

1. Consider each character in this cluster, and **evaluate** his or her relationship with nature. Then place them on a continuum chart such as the one below. Be prepared to explain your placement.

   Paul Bunyan ("The Growin' of Paul Bunyan")   *Oren Lyons ("Wisdomkeepers")*
   Johnny Appleseed ("The Growin' of Paul Bunyan")   *Ignacio Carrillo ("Nacho Loco")*

   protector   neutral   destroyer

2. Characters in "The Growin' of Paul Bunyan" speak in dialect. Some readers find this amusing; others are irritated by it. Did the dialect add to or subtract from your enjoyment of the story? Be prepared to explain your answer.

3. How do you think a person who relies on the lumber industry for a living would respond to "The Growin' of Paul Bunyan"?

4. How would the following people respond to the essay "Is Humanity a Special Threat?": the president of Exxon, a member of an environmental group such as Greenpeace, and Oren Lyons in "Wisdomkeepers"?

5. In the poem "Baptisms," the speaker says that some seek "dominion over rock and stream, ownership of forest and plain." How does an attitude of "dominion" or "ownership" affect how we manage our natural resources, in both good and bad ways?

6. Evaluate your relationship with nature; then place yourself on the continuum chart from question one and explain your placement.

Writing Activity: Position Paper

Pick one of the following quotations and write a position paper on why you agree or disagree with it.

> *". . . there's nobody bigger than a man who learns to grow."*
>
> —"The Growin' of Paul Bunyan"
>
> *"You don't fool around with Natural law and get away with it."*
>
> —"Wisdomkeepers"
>
> *"...the smartest thing they could have done after the [Exxon Valdez oil] spill is not one single thing."*
>
> —"Is Humanity a Special Threat?"

A Position Paper

- begins with a statement of the writer's opinion.
- uses examples to support the opinion.
- presents information clearly and logically.
- concludes by restating the writer's opinion.

CLUSTER TWO

What Happens When Humanity and Nature Collide?
Thinking Skill   ANALYZING

A Fable for Tomorrow

from *Silent Spring*

RACHEL CARSON

In 1962, the book Silent Spring *created a sensation. Its author, Rachel Carson, a biologist with the U.S. Bureau of Fisheries, warned the world about the dangers of pollution, especially from the wide use of chemicals. Carson was particularly concerned about DDT, a colorless, odorless insecticide that was considered almost a miracle after it was first introduced in the forties. By the sixties, however, Carson and other scientists noticed that DDT accumulates in ecosystems and has toxic effects on humans and animals. The title* Silent Spring *refers to the absence of birdsong, which Carson blamed on such poisons that kill or harm birds. The controversial book helped launch the environmental movement. What follows is an excerpt from this groundbreaking work.*

There was once a town in the heart of America where all life seemed to live in harmony with its surroundings. The town lay in the midst of a checkerboard of prosperous farms, with fields of grain and hillsides of orchards where, in spring, white clouds of bloom drifted above the green fields. In autumn, oak and maple and birch set up a blaze of color that flamed and flickered across a backdrop of pines. Then foxes barked in the hills and deer silently crossed the fields, half hidden in the mists of the fall mornings.

Along the roads, laurel, viburnum and alder,[1] great ferns and wildflowers delighted the traveler's eye through much of the year. Even in winter the

---

1 **laurel, viburnum and alder:** trees and shrubs

STONE CITY, IOWA (DETAIL)
1930
Grant Wood

roadsides were places of beauty, where countless birds came to feed on the berries and on the seed heads of the dried weeds rising above the snow. The countryside was, in fact, famous for the abundance and variety of its bird life, and when the flood of migrants was pouring through in spring and fall people traveled from great distances to observe them. Others came to fish the streams, which flowed clear and cold out of the hills and contained shady pools where trout lay. So it had been from the days many years ago when the first settlers raised their houses, sank their wells, and built their barns.

Then a strange blight crept over the area and everything began to change. Some evil spell had settled on the community: mysterious maladies swept the flocks of chickens; the cattle and sheep sickened and died. Everywhere was a shadow of death. The farmers spoke of much illness among their families. In the town the doctors had become more and more puzzled by new kinds of sickness appearing among their patients. There had been several sudden and unexplained deaths, not only among adults but even among children, who would be stricken suddenly while at play and die within a few hours.

There was a strange stillness. The birds, for example—where had they gone? Many people spoke of them, puzzled and disturbed. The feeding stations in the backyards were deserted. The few birds seen anywhere were moribund; they trembled violently and could not fly. It was a spring without voices. On the mornings that had once throbbed with the dawn chorus of robins, catbirds, doves, jays, wrens, and scores of other bird voices there was now no sound; only silence lay over the fields and woods and marsh.

On the farms the hens brooded, but no chicks hatched. The farmers complained that they were unable to raise any pigs—the litters were small and the young survived only a few days. The apple trees were coming into bloom but no bees droned among the blossoms, so there was no pollination and there would be no fruit.

The roadsides, once so attractive, were now lined with browned and withered vegetation as though swept by fire. These, too, were silent, deserted by all living things. Even the streams were now lifeless. Anglers[2] no longer visited them, for all the fish had died.

In the gutters under the eaves and between the shingles of the roofs, a white granular powder still showed a few patches; some weeks before it

---

2 **anglers:** people who fish

had fallen like snow upon the roofs and the lawns, the fields and streams.

No witchcraft, no enemy action had silenced the rebirth of new life in this stricken world. The people had done it themselves.

▲ ▲ ▲

This town does not actually exist, but it might easily have a thousand counterparts in America or elsewhere in the world. I know of no community that has experienced all the misfortunes I describe. Yet every one of these disasters has actually happened somewhere, and many real communities have already suffered a substantial number of them. A grim specter has crept upon us almost unnoticed, and this imagined tragedy may easily become a stark reality we all shall know. ∾

DUST BOWL   1933   Alexandre Hogue

Indian tribal leaders from the Amazon region of Ecuador arrive for a hearing in federal court in New York as plaintiffs in a billion-dollar class action lawsuit against Texaco, the American oil company.

Battle for the Rain Forest

JOE KANE

Deep in the Ecuadorian Amazon rain forest,[1] in a village more than a hundred miles from the nearest road, a young Cofan Indian named Bolivar smiles as he describes the day that his people finally stood up to their most powerful enemy—the oil companies.

The Cofan had always depended on the rain forest for everything—their food, clothing, and homes. Then, in 1972, Texaco began extracting oil from the Cofan homeland. Over the next 20 years, Texaco dumped billions of gallons of untreated toxic oil waste directly into the forest, creeks, and rivers on which the Cofan depended for their survival.

"Texaco poisoned everything," Bolivar says. He and his family and friends fled deeper into the forest. There they lived as before, until one day in November of 1991, when 24 employees of an American oil-exploration company marched into their new village and started cutting trees. The Cofan decided that they had had enough. "We had nowhere left to run," Bolivar says. "We had to fight back."

They took the oil workers prisoner and marched them out of the forest at spear point. They burned an oil well and destroyed a helicopter landing pad. When the Ecuadorian government sent in soldiers, the Cofan faced them down and backed them off. But the Cofan didn't stop there. They and 30,000 other residents of the Oriente (ore-ee-EN-tay), as the Ecuadorian Amazon is known, brought a lawsuit against Texaco, demanding more than a billion dollars for ruining their health, crops, and hunting and fishing lands. Filed in federal court in White Plains, New

---

1 **Ecuadorian Amazon rain forest:** the rain forest along the Amazon River in the South American country of Ecuador

York, where Texaco has its headquarters, the suit poses a fundamental question: Should American environmental and human-rights standards apply to U.S. companies operating overseas?

No Laws Protect Tribes

The suit has the potential to force U.S. oil companies to change the way they do business not only in Ecuador, but throughout the Amazon and, indeed, the world. Foreign oil now accounts for more than half the energy used in the United States, and giants such as Mobil, Occidental, Arco, and Oryx are pushing ever deeper into native territory in Venezuela, Colombia, Peru, and Ecuador. Under the laws of most South American countries, the native, or indigenous, people have no legal right to the oil beneath their homelands and no say in how it is extracted. Nor, for all practical purposes, are there any laws that control the environmental and human-rights consequences of oil production.

Increasingly, indigenous tribes that find themselves in the same predicament as the Cofan are taking matters into their own hands. In Peru, Machiguenga Indians recently forced Royal Dutch/Shell to abandon plans to develop a natural-gas field. In Colombia, the U'wa people threatened mass suicide if Occidental drilled for oil on their lands; in the face of worldwide negative publicity, Occidental recently scaled back its plans. In Ecuador, where the government has leased 85 percent of Amazon lands occupied by indigenous people to oil companies, Quichua Indians armed with machetes[2] and shotguns have shut down Arco wells. The Achuar are also battling Arco. And the Huaorani people—who are threatened with eradication of their culture for the sake of enough oil to meet U.S. energy needs for 10 days—have marched on Maxus Energy facilities.

These, however, are isolated battles in a much larger war. More typical is the agreement between Occidental and the Secoya, a tiny and isolated tribe. In exchange for signing a contract that enables the company to extract 155 million barrels of oil, Occidental gave the Secoya three stoves, three water pumps, some roofing material, an outboard motor, and three first-aid kits. Critics denounced the deal as "beads and trinkets," but the oil company defended it, saying the Secoya "have a very clear picture of what they want."

As they battle the oil companies, the indigenous people also find themselves battling national governments. Most of these countries are

2 **machetes:** large, heavy knives

impoverished and desperately need the oil revenue. In Ecuador, where 79 percent of the population lives in poverty, the government depends on oil for nearly half its revenues.

Nowhere are the consequences of this dilemma more profound than among the Cofan. When Texaco started taking oil out of the Oriente, it drilled 339 wells, blasted 18,000 miles of trails with dynamite, and cut 300 miles of roads. It built a pipeline that ruptured constantly, spilling more oil into the forest than was spilled in the worst ecological disaster in U.S. history, when the oil tanker *Exxon Valdez* ran aground off the coast of Alaska in 1989.

Texaco and its partner, Petro-ecuador, also dug hundreds of waste pits, into which they poured nearly all the toxic

South America

waste from the oil-extraction process, a practice that has long been outlawed in most of the U.S. The pits regularly leaked and washed out in the Oriente's heavy rains. By 1992, they had discharged more than 30 billion gallons of untreated waste directly into the creeks, rivers, and lakes that are the primary sources of drinking, bathing, and fishing water for the local people. When a team of researchers analyzed these waters in 1993, they found extremely high levels of poisons. These poisons are considered so deadly that the U.S. Environmental Protection agency says any amount at all poses a serious cancer risk.

Texaco says it broke no laws and has paid Ecuador $40 million for cleanup efforts. D. York LeCorgne, a former president of Texaco's Ecuadorian operations, says the waste pits "are not an inherent cause of pollution" and that pipeline spills were caused by acts of nature. According to LeCorgne, the company complied not only with Ecuadorian law, "but also with oil-industry standards of best practice and our own guiding principles and objectives, which affirm our commitment to the environment."

Critics charge that Texaco deliberately used substandard practices to maximize profits. The company broke no laws, they say, only because there were virtually no laws to break. On paper, Ecuador has laws that protect the Amazon's nature reserves, national parks, and indigenous people. But oil companies have told the government they won't tolerate any laws that might impede production, and the government has not enforced them. Furthermore, in a country considered one of the world's most corrupt, most of its oil revenues were allowed to be siphoned off by the oil companies and the small elite that controls the country.

POISONOUS SLUDGE

On a recent trip to the old Cofan hunting grounds, Bolivar points out a rusting metal pipe discharging poisonous sludge from a nearby oil well into a creek. The banks are coated with a film of oil, the trees along it are brown and lifeless, and the water itself smells like tar. Throughout the forest, dozens of creeks and lakes are in similar condition. Traditionally, the Cofan survived by hunting and gathering, and by growing a few staples such as bananas and manioc.[3] Their relationship with the forest was complex and highly sensitive—to make a blowgun and darts for hunting, for example, required more than 60 distinct forest products. But once Texaco came, Bolivar says, "we starved." He vividly recalls the day he managed to hunt and kill a sort of wild pig called a peccary, "but it was so soaked with oil that we could not eat it. We knew then that if we did not leave, we would die."

In biological terms, the Oriente is one of the richest places in the world; though no larger than Alabama, it is believed to be home to some 5 percent of all the species on the planet. In a single plot the size of two football fields, for example, researchers have identified 246 species of trees, more than are native to all of Western Europe. If cures for diseases such as AIDS and cancer were ever discovered, some researchers say, chances are they will come from the Oriente, or from the Amazonian region that surrounds it.

But as the Oriente is opened up for oil development, it suffers not only

3 **manioc:** plant with a root that yields an edible starch

from long-term pollution but from deforestation. Poor settlers from other parts of the country follow the oil roads into the rain forest, where they earn free title to land by "improving" it—in other words, by cutting down the trees and turning rain forest into farms. Often, these are lands that have long been occupied by indigenous people. Vast regions of the Oriente have already been destroyed, without any protection for their biological treasures.

Royal Dutch/Shell is expected to open an oil concession on the eastern side of the new Cofan lands, and Bolivar has little doubt that another round of confrontations will soon begin.

"We have no choice," he says. "This is our home." But as he has also come to learn, however painfully, it is a home intimately connected to a distant nation whose thirst for oil is second to none. ∾

Note: At the time of publication of this anthology (Fall 2000), the Cofan's lawsuit against Texaco had been pending for seven years. The issue of whether to try the case in the U.S. or Ecuador had not yet been decided.

A man measures the depth of oil refuse allegedly dumped by the Texaco oil company in the Oriente region of Ecuador.

All Revved Up About an
Even Bigger Vehicle

DAVE BARRY

If there's one thing this nation needs, it's bigger cars. That's why I'm
excited that Ford is coming out with a new mound o' metal that will offer
consumers even more total road-squatting mass than the current leader
in the humongous-car category, the popular Chevrolet Suburban
Subdivision, the first passenger automobile designed to be, right off the
assembly line, visible from the Moon.

I don't know what the new Ford will be called. Probably something
like the "Ford Untamed Wilderness Adventure." In the TV commercials,
it will be shown splashing through rivers, charging up rocky mountain-
sides, swinging on vines, diving off cliffs, racing through the surf and
fighting giant sharks hundreds of feet beneath the ocean surface—all the
daredevil things that cars do in Sport Utility Vehicle Commercial World,
where nobody ever drives on an actual road. In fact, the interstate high-
ways in Sport Utility Vehicle Commercial World, having been abandoned
by humans, are teeming with deer, squirrels, birds and other wildlife that
have fled from the forest to avoid being run over by nature-seekers in
multi-ton vehicles barreling through the underbrush at 50 miles per hour.

In the real world, of course, nobody drives Sport Utility Vehicles in the
forest, because when you have paid upward of $40,000 for a transporta-
tion investment, the last thing you want is squirrels pooping on it. No, if
you want a practical "off-road" vehicle, you get yourself a 1973 American
Motors Gremlin, which combines the advantage of not being worth

worrying about with the advantage of being so ugly that poisonous snakes flee from it in terror.

In the real world, what people mainly do with their Sport Utility Vehicles, as far as I can tell, is try to maneuver them into and out of parking spaces. I base this statement on my local supermarket, where many of the upscale patrons drive Chevrolet Subdivisions. I've noticed that these people often purchase just a couple of items—maybe a bottle of diet water and a two-ounce package of low-fat dried carrot shreds—which they put into the back of their Subdivisions, which have approximately the same cargo capacity, in cubic feet, as Finland. This means there is plenty of room left over back there in case, on the way home, these people decide to pick up something else, such as a herd of bison.

Then comes the scary part: getting the Subdivision out of the parking space. This is a challenge, because the driver apparently cannot, while sitting in the driver's seat, see all the way to either end of the vehicle. I drive a compact car, and on a number of occasions I have found myself trapped behind a Subdivision backing directly toward me, its massive metal butt looming high over my head, making me feel like a Tokyo pedestrian looking up at Godzilla.

I've tried honking my horn, but the Subdivision drivers can't hear me, because they're always talking on cellular phones the size of Chiclets. ("The Bigger Your Car, the Smaller Your Phone," that is their motto.) I don't know whom they're talking to. Maybe they're negotiating with their bison suppliers. Or maybe they're trying to contact somebody in the same area code as the rear ends of their cars, so they can find out what's going on back there. All I know is, I'm thinking of carrying marine flares, so I can fire them into the air as a warning to Subdivision drivers that they're about to run me over. Although frankly, I'm not sure they'd care if they did. A big reason why they bought a Sport Utility Vehicle is "safety," in the sense of, "you, personally, will be safe, although every now and then you may have to clean the remains of other motorists out of your wheel wells."

Anyway, now we have the new Ford, which will be *even larger* than the Subdivision, which I imagine means it will have separate decks for the various classes of passengers, and possibly, way up in front by the hood ornament, Leonardo DiCaprio showing Kate Winslet how to fly. I can't wait until one of these babies wheels into my supermarket parking lot. Other motorists and pedestrians will try to flee in terror, but they'll be sucked in by the Ford's powerful gravitational field and become stuck to its massive sides like so many refrigerator magnets. They won't be noticed, however, by the Ford's driver, who will be busy whacking at the side of his or her head, trying to dislodge his or her new cell phone, which is the size of a single grain of rice and has fallen deep into his or her ear canal.

And it will not stop there. This is America, darn it, and Chevrolet is not about to just sit by and watch Ford walk away with the coveted title of Least Sane Motor Vehicle. No, cars will keep getting bigger: I see a time, not too far from now, when upscale suburbanites will haul their overdue movies back to the video-rental store in full-size, 18-wheel tractor-trailers with names like "The Vagabond." It will be a proud time for all Americans, a time for us to cheer for our country. We should cheer loud, because we'll be hard to hear, inside the wheel wells. ❧

When Nature Comes Too Close

ANTHONY BRANDT

The quiet village of North Haven, N.Y., occupies a 2.5-square-mile peninsula connected to the South Fork of Long Island[1] by a spit of sand. The houses of its 733 residents are scattered about a landscape of meadows, ponds and oak forests. If you drive through North Haven quickly, you might never see a deer. And you might never know this is the hottest spot in what is rapidly becoming the war of the suburbs—the war between humans and wildlife.

Drive slowly through the village's back roads and you will see white-tailed deer in abundance, walking through the woods, feeding in people's yards. In an hour and a half I counted 30 deer. They did not startle at the sound of my car; sometimes they didn't even look up.

The deer population has been costly to North Haven's environment. In the woods the understory has disappeared; nothing grows below five feet off the ground. Small mammals and ground-nesting birds have vanished, their habitat destroyed. The woods cannot replenish themselves because the deer eat all the saplings. Three-fourths of the residents have had damage to their ornamental plantings; others have built eight-foot fences around their property. Mayor Bob Ratcliffe believes North Haven's ecosystem could handle about 60 deer. In the fall of 1996, the number stood at more than 600.

▲ ▲ ▲

1 **South Fork of Long Island:** the southern part of an island in southeast New York

Even more important: deer carry ticks (as many as 100 on each ear) that can transmit Lyme disease to people. The symptoms can include fatigue, a rash, fever, and muscle and joint pain. If not treated early, the disease can severely damage the central nervous system.

Ratcliffe would like the state to haul the deer someplace else. But where? Deer are thriving in suburbs all across the country; some wildlife biologists say the United States has as many as 20 million. Lyme disease cases run to more than 16,000 a year nationwide. There are hundreds of thousands of car-deer collisions every year, costing more than $70 million in damage.

It's not just deer, either. The situation in North Haven is indicative of a growing nationwide problem: the spread of wildlife into human habitats and vice versa. This is happening for a host of reasons, including population growth, changing hunting laws, a dearth of natural predators and shifting attitudes toward nature. "Animal populations are recovering strongly, and the suburbs are spreading into what was animal habitat," says Cornell University wildlife researcher Jody Enck. "It's likely to continue." While not yet a national crisis, in many areas it looks to become one as the local wildlife bring damage, disease and even danger to our own back yards.

Every animal carries its own set of problems. Canada geese, which defecate as frequently as every eight minutes, are fouling golf courses, parks and lawns all over the East and Midwest. Beavers are flooding roads and basements in New York, Minnesota and New England, causing thousands of dollars in damage. Raccoons spread rabies, and they love suburban living.

The larger animals, however, present the biggest threats. Mountain lions are appearing with increasing frequency in California suburbs, where one wandered into a shopping center; others were seen on school grounds. A mountain lion was also spotted near Minneapolis. The animals may even be returning to the Northeast, with sightings reported as far south as Connecticut.

Moose are expanding their range from northern New England south. In 1996 one appeared in the Delaware Water Gap on the Pennsylvania-New Jersey line. They can be major road hazards, as cars do not intimidate them. When your car strikes a moose, it sweeps the legs out from under the animal, resulting in 1000 pounds of meat and bone coming through the windshield into your lap. In northern New England the human-fatality rate in such collisions is about 25 times higher than in car-deer collisions.

▲ ▲ ▲

Bear proliferation, meanwhile, has taken place all across the country. In 1995 a black bear attacked a 14-year-old girl in her back yard in Monroe, Wash. Wisconsin wildlife agents handled 1000 calls in 1996 complaining about black bears. Bears have been sighted inside the city limits of Chattanooga and Pittsburgh, captured in the suburbs of New York City and Knoxville, and discovered on the outskirts of Orlando. In 1971 there were perhaps 20 or 30 bears in New Jersey; now the number is an estimated 550. In a western Massachusetts town, a black bear came through a screen door, grabbed a bag of candy bars off the kitchen table and fled.

It is the coyote, however, that constitutes the most widespread challenge to our ideas of where wildlife should live. Coyotes roam in every one of the 48 contiguous states and are by no means confined to rural areas. They have been seen in resort communities on barrier islands off the Atlantic Coast, and in the suburbs of Chicago, St. Louis and New York. A coyote den was found on the median strip of Route 128, which circles Boston. In Indiana the coyote population has increased from 500 in 1970 to more than 20,000 today.

No predatory mammal is as adaptable as the coyote. "It eats all types of food," notes Marc Bekoff, a professor of biology at the University of Colorado. That's putting it mildly. Mice, rabbits, birds, snakes, bats, iguanas, watermelon, sheep, goats, belts and belt buckles, fish, frogs, potatoes, berries—all have been found in coyote stomachs. What they consume depends on where they are. In the suburbs they eat garbage; the dumpster is one of their favorite sources. They also eat pets. Over an 18-month period in Benbrook, Texas, more than 50 cats disappeared, apparently killed by coyotes.

They are very hard to control. In the West, coyote eradication through bounties, poisoning and hunting has been unsuccessful. "They're very intelligent, very educable," says Robert Chambers, retired professor of wildlife biology at the State University of New York College of Environmental Science and Forestry. They're also difficult to trap, and more so the older and wilier they become.

▲ ▲ ▲

Few of us are easy in our conscience about this situation. Who does not admire the grace of the deer? The street smarts of the coyote?

But a black bear in our garbage can? Coyotes feeding on our beloved dog, Jack? That's a different story. Wild animals are supposed to be wild; they're supposed to keep their distance. They don't belong in our back yard. The very notion violates our ideas about the boundaries between the domestic and the wild.

No one has any easy answers. Michael Conover, director of the Berryman Institute at Utah State University, wonders, "How can we create a world that has the wildlife we all love and cherish, yet solve these specific problems with animals?" Conover is trying to find solutions without resorting to large-scale slaughter. "It's much better to solve the problem by changing the animals' behavior," he said.

When the deer problem became acute in North Haven, the community considered contraception, but the costs proved prohibitive. "The contraceptive is a vaccine derived from pig ovaries, and it must be administered by dart gun," explains Cornell University wildlife biologist Paul Curtis. "Each free-ranging deer must be tagged as a warning, to prevent human consumption of the vaccine. Just to capture and mark the animal is $200 per deer. Two doses of the vaccine per deer per year are necessary." In North Haven the cost would have been tens of thousands of dollars every year.

"We've had this huge investment in studying deer, geese and other animals from the extractive[2] perspective," says John Hadidian, who

2 **extractive:** removed but not replaced

directs the Urban Wildlife Protection Program of the Humane Society of the United States. "Now we need a whole new science to understand what the problems are in the suburbs—and to figure out what to do." Until then, he says, we have to learn to be more tolerant of local wildlife.

Meanwhile, we are finding that nature isn't just "out there" any longer, somewhere in Montana or the Amazon rain forest. It is staring at us with big, hungry eyes, right where our azaleas³ used to be. ∾

---

3 **azaleas:** ornamental bushes

A Sound of Thunder

RAY BRADBURY

The sign on the wall seemed to quaver under a film of sliding warm water. Eckels felt his eyelids blink over his stare, and the sign burned in this momentary darkness:

TIME SAFARI, INC.
SAFARIS TO ANY YEAR IN THE PAST.
YOU NAME THE ANIMAL.
WE TAKE YOU THERE.
YOU SHOOT IT.

A warm phlegm gathered in Eckels's throat; he swallowed and pushed it down. The muscles around his mouth formed a smile as he put his hand slowly out upon the air, and in that hand waved a check for ten thousand dollars to the man behind the desk.

"Does this safari guarantee I come back alive?"

"We guarantee nothing," said the official, "except the dinosaurs." He turned. "This is Mr. Travis, your Safari Guide in the Past. He'll tell you what and where to shoot. If he says no shooting, no shooting. If you dis-obey instructions, there's a stiff penalty of another ten thousand dollars, plus possible government action, on your return."

Eckels glanced across the vast office at a mass and tangle, a snaking and humming of wires and steel boxes, at an aurora that flickered now orange, now silver, now blue. There was a sound like a gigantic bonfire burning all of Time, all the years and all the parchment calendars, all the hours piled high and set aflame.

A touch of the hand and this burning would, on the instant, beautifully reverse itself. Eckels remembered the wording in the advertisements to the letter. Out of chars and ashes, out of dust and coals, like golden salamanders[1], the old years, the green years, might leap; roses sweeten the air, white hair turn Irish-black[2], wrinkles vanish; all, everything fly back to seed, flee death, rush down to their beginnings, suns rise in western skies and set in glorious easts, moons eat themselves opposite to the custom, all and everything cupping one in another like Chinese boxes, rabbits into hats, all and everything returning to the fresh death, the seed death, the green death, to the time before the beginning. A touch of a hand might do it, the merest touch of a hand.

"Unbelievable." Eckels breathed, the light of the Machine on his thin face. "A real Time Machine." He shook his head. "Makes you think. If the election had gone badly yesterday, I might be here now running away from the results. Thank God Keith won. He'll make a fine President of the United States."

"Yes," said the man behind the desk. "We're lucky. If Deutscher had gotten in, we'd have the worst kind of dictatorship. There's an anti-everything man for you, a militarist, anti-Christ, anti-human, anti-intellectual. People called us up, you know, joking but not joking. Said if Deutscher became President, they wanted to go live in 1942. Of course it's not our business to conduct escapes, but to form safaris. Anyway, Keith's President now. All you got to worry about is—"

"Shooting my dinosaur," Eckels finished it for him.

"A *Tyrannosaurus rex*. The Tyrant Lizard, the most incredible monster in history. Sign this release. Anything happens to you, we're not responsible. Those dinosaurs are hungry."

Eckels flushed angrily. "Trying to scare me!"

"Frankly, yes. We don't want anyone going who'll panic at the first shot. Six safari leaders were killed last year, and a dozen hunters. We're here to give you the severest thrill a *real* hunter ever asked for. Traveling you back sixty million years to bag the biggest game in all of Time. Your personal check's still there. Tear it up."

Mr. Eckels looked at the check. His fingers twitched.

"Good luck," said the man behind the desk. "Mr. Travis, he's all yours."

They moved silently across the room, taking their guns with them,

---

1 **salamanders:** amphibians that look like lizards

2 **Irish-black:** the color of hair some Irish people have

toward the Machine, toward the silver metal and the roaring light.

▲　▲　▲

First a day and then a night and then a day and then a night, then it was day-night-day-night-day. A week, a month, a year, a decade! A.D. 2055. A.D. 2019. 1999! 1957! Gone! The Machine roared.

They put on their oxygen helmets and tested the intercoms.

Eckels swayed on the padded seat, his face pale, his jaw stiff. He felt the trembling in his arms, and he looked down and found his hands tight on the new rifle. There were four other men in the Machine. Travis, the Safari Leader; his assistant, Lesperance; and two other hunters, Billings and Kramer. They sat looking at each other, and the years blazed around them.

"Can these guns get a dinosaur cold?" Eckels felt his mouth saying.

"If you hit them right," said Travis on the helmet radio. "Some dinosaurs have two brains, one in the head, another far down the spinal column. We stay away from those. That's stretching luck. Put your first two shots into the eyes, if you can, blind them, and go back into the brain."

The Machine howled. Time was a film run backwards. Suns fled and ten million moons fled after them. "Think," said Eckels. "Every hunter that ever lived would envy us today. This makes Africa seem like Illinois."

The Machine slowed; its scream fell to a murmur. The Machine stopped.

The sun stopped in the sky.

The fog that had enveloped the Machine blew away, and they were in an old time, a very old time indeed, three hunters and two Safari Heads with their blue metal guns across their knees.

"Christ isn't born yet," said Travis. "Moses has not gone to the mountain to talk with God. The Pyramids are still in the earth, waiting to be cut out and put up. *Remember* that. Alexander, Caesar, Napoleon, Hitler—none of them exists."

The man nodded.

"That"—Mr. Travis pointed—"is the jungle of sixty million, two thousand and fifty-five years before President Keith."

He indicated a metal path that struck off into green wilderness, over streaming swamp, among giant ferns and palms.

"And that," he said, "is the Path, laid by Time Safari for your use. It floats six inches above the earth. Doesn't touch so much as one grass blade, flower, or tree. It's an anti-gravity metal. Its purpose is to keep you from touching this world of the past in any way. Stay on the Path. Don't go off it. I repeat, *don't go off*. For *any* reason! If you fall off, there's a penalty. And don't shoot any animal we don't okay."

"Why?" asked Eckels.

They sat in the ancient wilderness. Far birds' cries blew on a wind, and the smell of tar and old salt sea, moist grasses, and flowers the color of blood.

"We don't want to change the Future. We don't belong here in the Past. The government doesn't *like* us here. We have to pay big graft[3] to keep our franchise.[4] A Time Machine is finicky business. Not knowing it, we might kill an important animal, a small bird, a roach, a flower even, thus destroying an important link in a growing species."

"That's not clear," said Eckels.

"All right," Travis continued, "say we accidentally kill one mouse here. That means all the future families of this one particular mouse are destroyed, right?"

"Right."

"And all the families of the families of the families of that one mouse! With a stamp of your foot, you annihilate first one, then a dozen, then a thousand, a million, a *billion* possible mice!"

"So they're dead," said Eckels. "So what?"

"So what?" Travis snorted quietly. "Well, what about the foxes that'll need those mice to survive? For want of ten mice, a fox dies. For want of ten foxes, a lion starves. For want of a lion, all manner of insects, vultures, infinite billions of life forms are thrown into chaos and destruction. Eventually it all boils down to this: fifty-nine million years later, a caveman, one of a dozen on the *entire world*, goes hunting wild boar or saber-toothed tiger for food. But you, friend, have *stepped* on all the tigers in that region. By stepping on *one* single mouse. So the caveman starves. And the caveman, please note, is not just *any* expendable man, no! He is an *entire future nation*. From his loins would have sprung ten sons. From *their* loins one hundred sons, and thus onward to a civilization. Destroy this one man, and you destroy a race, a people, an entire history of life. It is comparable to slaying some of Adam's grandchildren. The stomp of your

---

3 **graft:** the getting of money in dishonest ways; in this case bribes

4 **franchise:** right or license to operate a business in a particular place

foot, on one mouse, could start an earthquake, the effects of which could shake our earth and destinies down through Time to their very foundations. With the death of that one caveman, a billion others yet unborn are throttled in the womb. Perhaps Rome never rises on its seven hills. Perhaps Europe is forever a dark forest, and only Asia waxes healthy and teeming. Step on a mouse, and you crush the pyramids. Step on a mouse, and you leave your print, like a Grand Canyon, across Eternity. Queen Elizabeth might never be born, Washington might not cross the Delaware, there might never be a United States at all. So be careful. Stay on the Path. *Never* step off!"

"I see," said Eckels. "Then it wouldn't pay for us even to touch the *grass*?"

"Correct. Crushing certain plants could add up infinitesimally. A little error here could multiply in sixty million years, all out of proportion. Of course, maybe our theory is wrong. Maybe Time *can't* be changed by us. Or maybe it can be changed only in little, subtle ways. A dead mouse here makes an insect imbalance there, a population disproportion later, a bad harvest further on, a depression, mass starvation, and, finally, a change in *social* temperament in far-flung countries. Something much more subtle, like that. Perhaps only a soft breath, a whisper, a hair, pollen on the air, such a slight, slight change that unless you looked close you wouldn't see it. Who knows? Who really can say he knows? We don't know. We're guessing. But until we do know for certain whether our messing around in Time *can* make a big roar or a little rustle in history, we're being careful. This Machine, this Path, your clothing and bodies, were sterilized, as you know, before the journey. We wear these oxygen helmets so we can't introduce our bacteria into an ancient atmosphere."

"How do we know which animals to shoot?"

"They're marked with red paint," said Travis. "Today, before our journey, we sent Lesperance here back with the Machine. He came to this particular era and followed certain animals."

"Studying them?"

"Right," said Lesperance. "I track them through their entire existence, noting which of them lives longest. Very few. How many times they mate. Not often. Life's short. When I find one that's going to die when a tree falls on him, or one that drowns in a tar pit, I note the exact hour, minute, and second. I shoot a paint bomb. It leaves a red patch on his side. We can't miss it. Then I correlate our arrival in the Past so that we meet the monster not more than two minutes before he would have died anyway. This way, we kill only animals with no future, that are never going to mate again. You see how *careful* we are?"

"But if you came back this morning in Time," said Eckels eagerly, "you must've bumped into *us*, our Safari! How did it turn out? Was it successful? Did all of us get through—alive?"

Travis and Lesperance gave each other a look.

"That'd be a paradox," said the latter. "Time doesn't permit that sort of mess—a man meeting himself. When such occasions threaten, Time steps aside. Like an airplane hitting an air pocket. You felt the Machine jump just before we stopped? That was us passing ourselves on the way back to the Future. We saw nothing. There's no way of telling *if* this expedition was a success, *if* we got our monster, or whether all of us— meaning *you*, Mr. Eckels—got out alive."

Eckels smiled palely.

"Cut that," said Travis sharply. "Everyone on his feet!"

They were ready to leave the Machine.

The jungle was high and the jungle was broad and the jungle was the entire world forever and forever. Sounds like music and sounds like flying tents filled the sky, and those were pterodactyls soaring with cavernous gray wings, gigantic bats of delirium and night fever. Eckels, balanced on the narrow Path, aimed his rifle playfully.

"Stop that!" said Travis. "Don't even aim for fun, blast you! If your gun should go off—"

Eckels flushed. "Where's our *Tyrannosaurus*?"

Lesperance checked his wristwatch. "Up ahead. We'll bisect his trail in sixty seconds. Look for the red paint! Don't shoot till we give the word. Stay on the Path. *Stay on the Path!*"

They moved forward in the wind of morning.

"Strange," murmured Eckels. "Up ahead, sixty million years, Election Day over. Keith made President. Everyone celebrating. And here we are, a million years lost, and they don't exist. The things we worried about for months, a lifetime, not even born or thought of yet."

"Safety catches off, everyone!' ordered Travis. "You, first shot, Eckels. Second, Billings. Third, Kramer."

"I've hunted tiger, wild boar, buffalo, elephant, but now, this is *it*," said Eckels. "I'm shaking like a kid."

"Ah," said Travis.

Everyone stopped.

Travis raised his hand. "Ahead," he whispered. "In the mist. There he is. There's His Royal Majesty now."

The jungle was wide and full of twitterings, rustlings, murmurs, and sighs.

Suddenly it all ceased, as if someone had shut a door.

Silence.

A sound of thunder.

Out of the mist, one hundred yards away, came *Tyrannosaurus rex.*

"It," whispered Eckels. "It . . ."

"Sh!"

It came on great oiled, resilient, striding legs. It towered thirty feet above half of the trees, a great evil god, folding its delicate watchmaker's claws close to its oily, reptilian chest. Each lower leg was a piston, a thousand pounds of white bone, sunk in thick ropes of muscle, sheathed over in a gleam of pebbled skin like the mail of a terrible warrior. Each thigh was a ton of meat, ivory, and steel mesh. And from the great breathing cage of the upper body those two delicate arms dangled out front, arms with hands which might pick up and examine men like toys, while the snake neck coiled. And the head itself, a ton of sculptured stone, lifted easily upon the sky. Its mouth gaped, exposing a fence of teeth like daggers. Its eyes rolled, ostrich eggs, empty of all expression save hunger. It closed its mouth in a death grin. It ran, its pelvic bones crushing aside trees and bushes, its taloned feet clawing damp earth, leaving prints six inches deep wherever it settled its weight. It ran with a gliding ballet step, far too poised and balanced for its ten tons. It moved into a sunlit arena warily, its beautifully reptilian hands feeling the air.

"Why, why—" Eckels twitched his mouth. "It could reach up and grab the moon."

"Sh!" Travis jerked angrily. "He hasn't seen us yet."

"It can't be killed." Eckels pronounced this verdict quietly, as if there could be no argument. He had weighed the evidence and that was his considered opinion. The rifle in his hands seemed a cap gun. "We were fools to come. This is impossible."

"Shut up!' hissed Travis.

"Nightmare."

"Turn around," commanded Travis. "Walk quietly to the Machine. We'll remit one half your fee."

"I didn't realize it would be this *big,*" said Eckels. "I

miscalculated, that's all. And now I want out."

"It *sees* us!"

"There's the red paint on its chest!"

The Tyrant Lizard raised itself. Its armored flesh glittered like a thousand green coins. The coins, crusted with slime, steamed. In the slime, tiny insects wriggled, so that the entire body seemed to twitch and undulate, even while the monster itself did not move. It exhaled. The stink of raw flesh blew down the wilderness.

"Get me out of here," said Eckels. "It was never like this before. I was always sure I'd come through alive. I had good guides, good safaris and safety. This time, I figured wrong. I've met my match and admit it. This is too much for me to get hold of."

"Don't run," said Lesperance. "Turn around. Hide in the Machine."

"Yes," Eckels seemed to be numb. He looked at his feet as if trying to make them move. He gave a grunt of helplessness.

"Eckels!"

He took a few steps, blinking, shuffling.

"Not that way!"

The Monster, at the first motion, lunged forward with a terrible scream. It covered one hundred yards in six seconds. The rifles jerked up and blazed fire. A windstorm from the beast's mouth engulfed them in the stench of slime and old blood. The monster roared, teeth glittering with sun.

Eckels, not looking back, walking blindly to the edge of the Path, his gun limp in his arm, stepped off the Path and walked, not knowing it, in the jungle. His feet sank into green moss. His legs moved him, and he felt alone and remote from the events behind.

The rifles cracked again. Their sound was lost in shriek and lizard thunder. The great level of the reptile's tail swung up, lashed sideways. Trees exploded in clouds of leaf and branch. The Monster twitched its jeweler's hands down to fondle at the men, to twist them in half, to crush them like berries, to cram them into its teeth and its screaming throat. Its boulder-stone eyes leveled with the men. They saw themselves mirrored. They fired at the metallic eyelids and blazing black irises.

Like a stone idol, like a mountain avalanche, *Tyrannosaurus* fell. Thundering, it clutched trees, pulled them with it. It wrenched and tore the metal Path. The men flung themselves back and away. The body hit, ten tons of cold flesh and stone. The guns fired. The Monster lashed its armored tail, twitched its snake jaws and lay still. A fount of blood spurted from its throat. Somewhere inside, a sac of fluid burst. Sickening gushes drenched the hunters. They stood, red and glistening.

The thunder faded.

The jungle was silent. After the avalanche, a green peace. After the nightmare, morning.

Billings and Kramer sat on the pathway and threw up. Travis and Lesperance stood with smoking rifles, cursing steadily.

In the Time Machine, on his face, Eckels lay shivering. He had found his way back to the Path, climbed into the Machine.

Travis came walking, glanced at Eckels, took cotton gauze from a metal box and returned to the others, who were sitting on the Path.

"Clean up."

They wiped the blood from their helmets. They began to curse too. The Monster lay, a hill of solid flesh. Within, you could hear the sighs and murmurs as the farthest chambers of it died, the organs malfunctioning, liquids running a final instant from pocket to sac to spleen[5], everything shutting off, closing up forever. It was like standing by a wrecked locomotive or a steam shovel at quitting time, all valves being released or levered tight. Bones cracked; the tonnage of its own flesh, off balance, dead weight, snapped the delicate forearms, caught underneath. The meat settled, quivering.

Another cracking sound. Overhead, a gigantic tree branch broke from its heavy mooring, fell. It crashed upon the dead beast with finality.

"There." Lesperance checked his watch. "Right on time. That's the giant tree that was scheduled to fall and kill this animal originally." He glanced at the two hunters. "You want the trophy picture?"

"What?"

"We can't take a trophy back to the Future. The body has to stay right where it would have died originally, so the insects, birds, and bacteria can get at it, as they were intended to. Everything in balance. The body stays. But we *can* take a picture of you standing near it."

The two men tried to think, but gave up, shaking their heads.

They let themselves be led along the metal Path. They sank wearily into the machine cushions. They gazed back at the ruined Monster, the stagnating mound, where already strange reptilian birds and golden insects were busy at the steaming armor.

| 5 **sac; spleen:** a pouch containing bodily fluid or an organ; an abdominal organ

A sound on the floor of the Time Machine stiffened them. Eckels sat there, shivering.

"I'm sorry," he said at last.

"Get up!" cried Travis.

Eckels got up.

"Go out on that Path alone," said Travis. He had his rifle pointed. "You're not coming back in the Machine. We're leaving you here!"

Lesperance seized Travis's arm. "Wait—"

"Stay out of this!" Travis shook his hand away. "This fool nearly killed us. But it isn't *that* so much, no. It's his *shoes*! Look at them! He ran off the Path. That *ruins* us! We'll forfeit! Thousands of dollars of insurance! We guaranteed no one leaves the Path. He left it. Oh, the fool! I'll have to report to the government. They might revoke our license to travel. Who knows *what* he's done to Time, to History!"

"Take it easy. All he did was kick up some dirt."

"How do we *know*?" cried Travis. "We don't know anything! It's all a mystery! Get out of here, Eckels!"

Eckels fumbled his shirt. "I'll pay anything. A hundred thousand dollars!"

Travis glared at Eckels's checkbook and spat. "Go out there. The Monster's next to the Path. Stick your arms up to your elbows in his mouth. Then you can come back with us."

"That's unreasonable!"

"The Monster's dead, you idiot. The bullets! The bullets can't be left behind. They don't belong in the Past; they might change anything. Here's my knife. Dig them out!"

The jungle was alive again, full of the old tremorings and bird cries. Eckels turned slowly to regard the primeval garbage dump, that hill of nightmares and terror. After a long time, like a sleepwalker he shuffled out along the Path.

He returned, shuddering, five minutes later, his arms soaked and red to the elbow. He turned out his hands. Each held a number of steel bullets. Then he fell. He lay where he fell, not moving.

"You didn't have to make him do that," said Lesperance.

"Didn't I? It's too early to tell." Travis nudged the still body. "He'll live. Next time he won't go hunting game like this. Okay." He jerked his thumb wearily at Lesperance. "Switch on. Let's go home."

1492. 1776. 1812.

They cleaned their hands and faces. They changed their caking shirts and pants. Eckels was up and around again, not speaking. Travis glared at him for a full ten minutes.

"Don't look at me," cried Eckels. "I haven't done anything."

"Who can tell?"

"Just ran off the Path, that's all, a little mud on my shoes—what do you want me to do, get down and pray?"

"We might need it. I'm warning you, Eckels, I might kill you yet. I've got my gun ready."

"I'm innocent. I've done nothing!"

1999. 2000. 2055.

The Machine stopped.

"Get out," said Travis.

The room was there as they had left it. But not the same as they had left it. The same man sat behind the same desk. But the same man did not quite sit behind the same desk.

Travis looked around swiftly. "Everything okay here?" he snapped.

"Fine. Welcome home!"

Travis did not relax. He seemed to be looking at the very atoms of the air itself, at the way the sun poured through the one high window.

"Okay, Eckels, get out. Don't ever come back."

Eckels could not move.

"You heard me," said Travis. "What're you *staring* at?"

Eckels stood smelling of the air, and there was a thing to the air, a chemical taint so subtle, so slight, that only a faint cry of his subliminal senses warned him it was there.

The colors, white, gray, blue, orange, in the wall, in the furniture, in the sky beyond the window, were . . . were . . . And there was a *feel*. His flesh twitched. His hands twitched. He stood drinking the oddness with the pores of his body. Somewhere, someone must have been screaming one of those whistles that only a dog can hear. His body screamed silence in return. Beyond this room, beyond this wall, beyond this man who was not quite the same man seated at this desk that was not quite the same desk . . . lay an entire world of streets and people. What sort of world it was now, there was no telling. He could feel them moving there, beyond the walls, almost, like so many chess pieces blown in a dry wind. . . .

But the immediate thing was the sign painted on the office wall, the same sign he had read earlier today on first entering.

Somehow, the sign had changed.

TYME SEFARI INC.
SEFARIS TU ANY YEER EN THE PAST.
YU NAIM THE ANIMALL.
WEE TAEKYUTHAIR.
YU SHOOT ITT.

Eckels felt himself fall into the chair. He fumbled crazily at the thick slime on his boots. He held up a clod of dirt, trembling. "No, it *can't* be. Not a *little* thing like that. No!"

Embedded in the mud, glistening green and gold and black, was a butterfly, very beautiful and very dead.

"Not a little thing like *that!* Not a butterfly!" cried Eckels.

It fell to the floor, an exquisite thing, a small thing that could upset balances and knock down a line of small dominoes and then big dominoes and then gigantic dominoes, all down the years across Time. Eckels's mind whirled. It *couldn't* change things. Killing one butterfly couldn't be *that* important! Could it?

His face was cold. His mouth trembled, asking: "Who—who won the presidential election yesterday?"

The man behind the desk laughed. "You joking? You know very well. Deutscher, of course! Who else? Not that fool weakling Keith. We got an iron man now, a man with guts!" The official stopped. "What's wrong?"

Eckels moaned. He dropped to his knees. He scrabbled at the golden butterfly with shaking fingers. "Can't we," he pleaded to the world, to himself, to the officials, to the Machine, "can't we take it *back*, can't we *make* it alive again? Can't we start over? Can't we—"

He did not move. Eyes shut, he waited, shivering. He heard Travis breathe loud in the room; he heard Travis shift his rifle, click the safety catch and raise the weapon.

There was a sound of thunder. ∾

And They Lived Happily Ever After for a While

JOHN CIARDI

It was down by the Dirty River
   As the Smog was beginning to thin
Because we had been so busy
   Breathing the worst of it in,

That the worst remained inside us
   And whatever we breathed back
Was only—sort of—grayish,
   Or at least not entirely black.

It was down by the Dirty River
   That flows to the Sticky Sea
I gave my heart to my Bonnie,
   And she gave hers to me.

I coughed, "I love you, Bonnie
   And do you love me true?"
The tears of joy flowed from my eyes
   When she sneezed back: "Yes—Achoo!"

It was high in the Garbage Mountains,
   In Saint Snivens by the Scent,
I married my darling Bonnie
   And we built our Oxygen Tent.

And here till the tanks are empty
   We sit and watch TV
And dream of the Dirty River
   On its way to the Sticky Sea.

Here till the needles quiver
   Shut on the zero mark
We sit hand in hand while the TV screen
   Shines like a moon in the dark.

I cough: "I love you, Bonnie.
   And do you love me true?"
And tears of joy flow from our eyes
   When she sneezes: "Yes—Achoo!"

Responding to Cluster Two

What Happens When Humanity and Nature Collide?

Thinking Skill ANALYZING

1. Using a chart such as the one below, **analyze** what happens in each of the following selections when humanity and nature collide. An example has been done for you.

Selection	Description of Collision	Result
A Fable for Tomorrow	*man-made chemicals cause death of ecosystem*	
Battle for the Rain Forest		
When Nature Comes Too Close		
All Revved Up About an Even Bigger Vehicle		
A Sound of Thunder		

2. In your opinion, what is the main point of "Battle for the Rain Forest"? **Analyzing** the needs and positions of native people, their governments, and foreign oil companies will help you decide.

3. Discuss the debate topic: "American environmental and human-rights standards should apply to U.S. companies operating overseas."

4. The tone of a piece of writing is its mood or atmosphere. In "Wisdomkeepers" in Cluster One, Oren Lyons conveys his philosophy in an angry tone. In one word each, how would you describe the tone of each selection in this cluster?

5. How does "A Sound of Thunder" illustrate "chaos theory" as it is described in the essay "Butterfly or Asteroid" on p. 9?

Writing Activity: Environmental Analysis

Of the environmental issues explored in this cluster, choose the one that matters to you most. **Analyze** why it is important and how it could be resolved.

A Strong Analysis

- demonstrates careful examination of each part of the topic.
- supports each point with evidence.
- organizes information clearly.
- ends with a summary of the ideas presented.

CLUSTER THREE

How Can We Live in Harmony with Nature?

Thinking Skill   PROBLEM SOLVING

Heroes for the Planet
Then and Now

WASTE DISPOSAL THEN

Garbage dumps used to allow anything and everything. Residents and businesses threw out both recyclable and nonrecyclable items, which were simply thrown away in the hopes that time and the elements would decompose at least some of the debris.

WASTE DISPOSAL NOW

Modern trash disposal often requires separation of recyclable items from biodegradable and hazardous wastes. Glass, metal, paper and certain types of plastics are transported to be turned into new products, while hazardous items such as batteries and solvents are processed at specially designed dump sites.

CAVEAT[1]

Recycled waste still only accounts for a tiny percentage of the total solid waste disposed each year. In the United States alone, an estimated 360 million tons of solid wastes—more than a ton and a half for each person— are generated in the residential and industrial sectors each year.

1 **caveat:** warning

FORESTRY THEN

Clear-cutting and hauling left hills denuded and scarred by logging roads. The lack of vegetation led to soil erosion and the muddying of upland rivers and streams.

FORESTRY NOW

Many wood-product companies practice sustainable forestry, where trees are planted for re-growth as soon as logging is completed.

CAVEAT

Trees grown in reforestation efforts are often a single species, which diminishes the area's biodiversity. Meanwhile, in many developing countries—where short-term economic concerns often outweigh efforts at long-term planning—forests are clear cut for cash or farmlands, without any attempt at reforestation.

The Sun

MARY OLIVER

Have you ever seen
anything
in your life
more wonderful

than the way the sun,
every evening,
relaxed and easy,
floats toward the horizon

and into the clouds or the hills,
or the rumpled sea,
and is gone—
and how it slides again

out of the blackness,
every morning,
on the other side of the world,
like a red flower

streaming upward on its heavenly oils,
say, on a morning in early summer,
at its perfect imperial distance—
and have you ever felt for anything

such wild love—
do you think there is anywhere, in any language,
a word billowing enough
for the pleasure

that fills you,
as the sun
reaches out,
as it warms you

as you stand there,
empty-handed—
or have you too
turned from this world—

or have you too
gone crazy
for power,
for things?

A Palace of Bird Beaks
a Folk Tale from the Yemen[1] Oral Tradition

RETOLD BY HOWARD SCHWARTZ AND BARBARA RUSH

There once was a king named Solomon, who was known throughout the world for his wisdom. Why, he could command the winds and birds to come whenever he called them. He even knew the language of every bird and animal on earth.

Now it so happened that King Solomon's wife was soon to have a birthday. The king asked her what gift she would like.

"Oh, I would like something that no other queen on earth has ever had," she said. "Build me a palace of bird beaks!"

And out of love for his wife, Solomon answered, "You shall have it, my dear. A palace of bird beaks shall be yours."

Then King Solomon called forth all the birds in the world and ordered them to come to his palace, prepared to give up their beaks. Before even a day had gone by, thousands of birds filled the sky, beating their wings and swooping down to the palace. All came: the strong eagle, the tiny hummingbird, the bluebird, the mockingbird, and every bird that lived on earth. The birds were not very happy at having to give up their beaks. But what could they do? They were among the smallest creatures in the kingdom. Soon every bird had flocked to the palace except one—the hoopoe[2]—a little bird with colorful feathers and a fine, pointed beak. As time passed and it did not arrive, the king became angry.

1 **Yemen:** Southern Arabic
2 **hoopoe:** an Old World bird with a crest and a slender bill

"Fetch the hoopoe and bring it here!" he shouted to his servants. "Let it be punished for failing to obey the king!"

At last the hoopoe was brought before the king.

"Where have you been?" King Solomon demanded. "Why have you kept me waiting?"

"Please, your Majesty, do not be angry with me," said the hoopoe. "I have been flying to the ends of the earth. I have seen gardens, forests, oceans, deserts—and from all that I have seen, I have gained much wisdom, so that I may serve you well. Punish me if you must, but first give me a chance to prove that I have not just been flying lazily about. Let me ask you three riddles. If you can answer correctly, then do what you will with me. But if there is even one of them that you cannot answer, then spare my life."

The other birds gasped. How shocked they were that a bird dared bargain with the king! But King Solomon admired this bold little creature, and he accepted the challenge. "Very well," he said, "ask your riddles. After all, how can your wisdom be compared to the wisdom of a king?"

So the hoopoe spoke. "This is the first riddle. Tell me, your Majesty, who is it who was never born and has never died?"

The king did not even pause to think.

"The Lord of the world, blessed be He," he said at once. And as he spoke, King Solomon thought, The Lord of the world who created all creatures to be free.

The hoopoe continued. "Here is the second riddle. Tell me, your Majesty, what water never rises from the ground and never falls from the sky?"

King Solomon smiled, for he knew the answer. "The answer is a tear," he said, "a tear that falls from an eye that cries with sadness." And as he finished answering, King Solomon looked around and saw all those birds stretched out before him, waiting sadly and helplessly for their beaks to be cut off. The king too was saddened, and a tear came to his eye.

Now a strange thing happened. Although King Solomon was certain that his wisdom was perfect, for just a moment it occurred to him that perhaps he had done a foolish thing in agreeing to build a palace of bird beaks.

Then the hoopoe spoke again, and this time it trembled, for it had only one riddle left—only one more chance to save itself.

"Your Majesty, what is it that is delicate enough to put food in a baby's mouth, yet strong enough to bore holes in the hardest wood?"

It did not take King Solomon long to reply. "Why, a bird's beak, of course!" he answered. And looking around at that great gathering of birds, he realized how special those creatures were, and how very precious their beaks were to them.

Meanwhile the hoopoe bowed its head. "Punish me as you will, your Majesty, for you have answered my three riddles." And it waited in silence to hear the harsh punishment of the king.

But the king was smiling. "Dear hoopoe," he announced in a loud voice, so that all the birds could hear, "I am known throughout the world for my wisdom, yet you are the one who is truly wise. You have shown me that a king should never be too proud to admit he has made a mistake. I have decided not to build a palace of bird beaks after all!"

At this, all the birds wanted to flap their wings in joy, but they did not dare to interrupt the king.

"For your wisdom you shall be rewarded, not punished," said King Solomon. He called forth the royal jeweler and bade him make the bird a small crown, much like the crown that he himself, the king, wore upon his head. And when the crown was finished, King Solomon placed it upon the head of the hoopoe.

So it is that to this day the hoopoe wears a crown on its forehead, to remind all the birds who see it of the reward of King Solomon and the wisdom of the bird who saved their beaks. ❧

The Face of a Spider

DAVID QUAMMEN

One evening a few years ago I walked back into my office after dinner and found roughly a hundred black widow spiders frolicking on my desk. I am not speaking metaphorically and I am not making this up: a hundred black widows. It was a vision of ghastly, breathtaking beauty, and it brought on me a wave of nausea. It also brought on a small moral crisis—one that I dealt with briskly, maybe rashly, in the dizziness of the moment, and that I've been turning back over in my mind ever since. I won't say I'm haunted by those hundred black widows, but I do remember them vividly. To me, they stand for something. They stand, in their small synedochical[1] way, for a large and important question.

The question is, How should a human behave toward the members of other living species?

A hundred black widows probably sounds like a lot. It is—even for Tucson, Arizona, where I was living then, a habitat in which black widows breed like rabbits and prosper like cockroaches, the females of the species growing plump as huckleberries and stringing their ragged webs in every free corner of every old shed and basement window. In Tucson, during the height of the season, a person can always on short notice round up eight or ten big, robust black widows, if that's what a person wants to do. But a hundred in one room? So all right, yes, there was a catch: These in my office were newborn babies.

---

1 **synecdochical:** symbolic. Synechdochy means the part that represents the whole.

A hundred scuttering bambinos,[2] each one no bigger than a poppy-seed. Too small still for red hourglasses, too small even for red egg timers. They had the aesthetic[3] virtue of being so tiny that even a person of good eyesight and patient disposition could not make out their hideous little faces.

Their mother had sneaked in when the rains began and set up a web in the corner beside my desk. I knew she was there—I got a reminder every time I dropped a pencil and went groping for it, jerking my hand back at the first touch of that distinctive, dry, high-strength web. But I hadn't made the necessary decision about dealing with her. I knew she would have to be either murdered or else captured adroitly in a pickle jar for relocation to the wild, and I didn't especially want to do either. (I had already squashed scores of black widows during those Tucson years but by this time, I guess, I was going soft.) In the meantime, she had gotten pregnant. She had laid her eggs into a silken egg sac the size of a Milk Dud and then protected that sac vigilantly, keeping it warm, fending off any threats, as black widow mothers do. While she was waiting for the eggs to come to term, she would have been particularly edgy, particularly unforgiving, and my hand would have been in particular danger each time I reached for a fallen pencil. Then the great day arrived. The spiderlings hatched from their individual eggs, chewed their way out of the sac, and started crawling, brothers and sisters together up toward the orange tensor lamp that was giving off heat and light on the desk of the nitwit who was their landlord.

By the time I stumbled in, fifty or sixty of them had reached the lampshade and rappelled back down on dainty silk lines, leaving a net of gossamer rigging between the lamp and the Darwin book (it happened to be an old edition of *Insectivorous Plants*, with marbled endpapers) that sat on the desk. Some dozen of others had already managed dispersal flights, letting out strands of buoyant silk and ballooning away on the rising air, as spiderlings do—in this case dispersing as far as the bookshelves. It was too late for one man to face one spider with just a pickle jar and an index card and his two shaky hands. By now I was proprietor of a highly successful black widow hatchery.

And the question was, How should a human behave toward the members of other living species?

---

2 **bambinos:** Italian for "children"

3 **aesthetic:** pleasing to the senses

▲   ▲   ▲

The Jain religion of India has a strong teaching on that question. The Sanskrit[4] word is *ahimsa*, generally rendered in English as "noninjury" or the imperative "do no harm." *Ahimsa* is the ethical centerpiece of Jainism, an absolute stricture against the killing of living beings—any living beings— and it led the traditional Jains to some extreme forms of observance. A rigorously devout Jain would burn no candles or lights, for instance, if there was danger a moth might fly into them. The Jain would light no fire for heating or cooking, again because it might cause the death of insects. He would cover his mouth and nose with a cloth mask, so as not to inhale any gnats. He would refrain from cutting his hair, on the grounds that the lice hiding in there might be gruesomely injured by the scissors. He could not plow a field, for fear of mutilating worms. He could not work as a carpenter or a mason, with all that dangerous sawing and crunching, nor could he engage in most types of industrial production. Consequently the traditional Jains formed a distinct socioeconomic class, composed almost entirely of monks and merchants. Their ethical canon[5] was not without what you and I might take to be glaring contradictions (vegetarianism was sanctioned, plants as usual getting dismissive treatment in the matter of rights to life), but at least they took it seriously. They lived by it. They tried their best to do no harm.

And this in a country, remember, where 10,000 humans died every year from snakebite, almost a million more from malaria carried in the bites of mosquitoes. The black widow spider, compared to these fellow creatures, seems a harmless and innocent beast.

But personally I hold no brief[6] for *ahimsa*, because I don't delude myself that it's even theoretically (let alone practically) possible. The basic processes of animal life, human or otherwise, do necessarily entail a fair bit of ruthless squashing and gobbling. Plants can sustain themselves on no more than sunlight and beauty and a hydroponic[7] diet—but not we animals. I've only mentioned this Jainist ideal to suggest the range of possible viewpoints . . .

. . . I have my own little notion of one measure that might usefully be applied in our relations with other species, and I offer it here seriously

---

4 **Sanskrit:** the classical language of India and Hinduism

5 **canon:** set of rules

6 **brief:** argument

7 **hydroponic:** water-based. Hydroponic farming uses nutrient-rich water in the place of soil.

despite the fact that it will probably sound godawful stupid.

Eye contact.

Make eye contact with the beast, the Other, before you decide upon action. No kidding, now, I mean get down on your hands and knees right there in the vegetable garden, and look that snail in the face. Lock eyes with that bull snake. Trade stares with the carp. Gaze for a moment into the many-faceted eyes—the windows to its soul—of the house fly, as it licks its way innocently across your kitchen counter. Look for signs of embarrassment or rancor or guilt. Repeat the following formula silently, like a mantra: "This is some mother's darling, this is some mother's child." *Then* kill if you will, or if it seems you must.

I've been experimenting with the eye-contact approach for some time myself. I don't claim that it has made me gentle or holy or put me in tune with the cosmic hum, but definitely it has been interesting. The hardest cases—and therefore I think the most telling—are the spiders.

▲   ▲   ▲

The face of a spider is unlike anything else a human will ever see. The word "ugly" doesn't even begin to serve. "Grotesque" and "menacing" are too mild. The only adequate way of communicating the effect of a spiderly countenance is to warn that it is "very different," and then offer a photograph. This trick should not be pulled on loved ones just before bedtime or when trying to persuade them to accompany you to the Amazon.

The special repugnant power of the spider physiognomy[8] derives, I think, from fangs and eyes. The former are too big and the latter are too many. But the fangs (actually the fangs are only terminal barbs on the *chelicerae,* as the real jaw limbs are called) need to be large, because all spiders are predators yet they have no pincers like a lobster or a scorpion, no talons like an eagle, no social behavior like a pack of wolves. Large clasping fangs armed with poison glands are just their required equipment for earning a living. And what about those eight eyes—big ones and little ones, arranged in two rows, all bugged-out and pointing everywhichway? (My wife the biologist offers a theory here: "They have an eye for each leg, like us—so they don't *step* in anything.") Well, a predator does need good eyesight, binocular focus, peripheral vision. Sensory perception is crucial to any animal that lives by the hunt and, unlike insects, arachnids possess no antennae. Beyond that, I don't know. I don't *know* why a spider has eight eyes.

8 **physiognomy:** outward appearance

I only know that, when I make eye contact with one, I feel a deep physical shudder of revulsion, and of fear, and of fascination; and I am reminded that the human style of face is only one accidental pattern among many, some of the others being quite different. I remember that we aren't alone. I remember that we are the norm of goodness and comeliness only to ourselves. I wonder about how ugly I look to the spider.

▲ ▲ ▲

The hundred baby black widows on my desk were too tiny for eye contact. They were too numerous, it seemed, to be gathered one by one into a pickle jar and carried to freedom in the backyard. I killed them all with a can of Raid. I confess to that slaughter with more resignation than shame, the jostling struggle for life and space being what it is. I can't swear I would do differently today. But there is this lingering suspicion that I squandered an opportunity for some sort of moral growth.

I still keep their dead and dried mother, and their vacated egg sac, in a plastic vial on an office shelf. It is supposed to remind me of something or other.

And the question continues to puzzle me: How should a human behave toward the members of other living species?

Last week I tried to make eye contact with a tarantula. This was a huge specimen, all hairy and handsomely colored, with a body as big as a hamster and legs the size of Bic pens. I ogled it through a sheet of plate glass. I smiled and winked. But the animal hid its face in distrust. ∞

This essay has been modified from the original.

David Meets Goliath at City Hall

A N D R E W H O L L E M A N

"Mom, I've got to go to the library. Can you drive me?" That was the first thing I said after I read a registered letter that my parents got. It concerned the development of land near my home and stated that a meeting about it would be held at the town hall.

It made me mad. "How could this be happening?" I asked myself. I knew these woods—I had loved, studied, explored them; I practically grew up there. Now an $11 million, 180-unit condominium complex was going to be built on one privately owned parcel (sandwiched between two pieces of preserved conservation land). That parcel was almost half wetlands. It contained wood turtles, blue-spotted salamanders (both declining species rated "of special concern" by wildlife authorities), great blue herons, various hawks, lady's-slippers, and mountain laurel.[1]

I was angry because this beautiful piece of land and wildlife habitat was about to be destroyed. Weren't people aware of their environment after being informed every day from so many sources that our world is at stake?

I also had so many memories based in that area. When I was very young, I took nature walks there with my family and even remember having a winter picnic in the snow by a stream with them. Later, when I was older, I went there with my friend on our own nature walks or to go ice-skating on a pond in the woods.

---

1 **blue-spotted salamanders; lady's-slippers; mountain laurel:** amphibians;
   orchids; flowering shrubs

Now I go there to sit and think for hours on end. There are times I just sit and watch the deer, fox, and other animals. I go fishing sometimes in the ice-skating pond and have caught a twelve-inch bass (this is not a fish story).

I guess I was just plain angry that "my land" was going to be destroyed and that it was one more insult to the environment. I had to do something.

At the library, I looked up the Hatch Act, the Massachusetts law that protects wetlands. I also read the town Master Plan. It listed the acreage of the site and noted which parts were wetland, poor soil, or developable. There I found the ammunition I needed: Only 2.2 acres of the 16.3-acre site were considered sound enough to be developed.

After leaving the library, I wrote a petition and took it to neighbors to get signatures from registered voters and to tell people about the developer's meeting and the harm that this complex could do to our woods.

Much to my surprise, most people showed a lot of interest and were happy to sign. I collected about 150 signatures (only two adults said no) and also started a petition for students to sign.

It wasn't always easy going from door to door. One day, while crossing my beloved wetlands to reach another part of the neighborhood, I slipped on a rotted log and sent myself and the petition flying into a small, muddy stream. It took a while for the petition to dry and for my mother to iron out the papers. That was the last time I went through the swamp with anything important that wasn't waterproofed.

▲　▲　▲

When the night came for the meeting, my parents and I were directed to a room that could hold about 50 people (the developer had sent his original notification to the 50 families whose homes abutted the property). Within twenty minutes we were moved to a larger room in the town hall because it was obvious that many more people would show up. Finally, it became apparent that we needed a larger room still.

A half hour later, more than 250 people had gathered in the hall's basement gymnasium, ready to hear about the proposed project and its impact on our community. A number of times during the meeting, the developer took credit for inviting the people there to hear about his proposal. The crowd, just as often, reminded him that I was the one who had actually invited most of them.

After the developer discussed his project plans, I made my speech. You can't have stage fright at a moment like this—you have to just get up and tell your side of the story. Holding the shell of a wood turtle I'd found in the woods, I spoke about how this development would destroy the animal and plant life. I told how the stream on the land would eventually become polluted and carry its pollution into nearby town wells. I also suggested another site the developer might use, one that would better withstand the environmental impact. (Interestingly enough, the developer has already started constructing a condominium on the alternative site that I had originally suggested. It was the old drive-in movie lot here in town.)

After that night, I wrote letters to many state representatives and senators and also to a local TV anchorwoman, hoping to gain more support. I included my petition in the letters. I then telephoned the Massachusetts Audubon Society "Helpline" and spoke with Dr. Dorothy Arvidson, a biologist and now a good friend.

She told me to keep my fight local, that I should approach the town representatives because national and state organizations wouldn't be much help. She was telling me other things to do when I interrupted to say I was only twelve years old. "Well, that's no excuse," she said, and went on giving me information.

From that point on, meetings were held every week for seven months so the developer could present his proposal to conservation commissions, appeal boards, and selectmen[2]—just to name a few. These meetings often took place on school nights and sometimes lasted up to three and a half hours. Somehow I managed to attend every one and still get good grades.

Later we formed a neighborhood association to keep people up-to-date and to raise money for a lawyer and an environmental scientist. My dad and I became members of the Concord Road Neighborhood Association. The public supported us, donating nearly $16,000 to stop the condominium project.

I was told that "you can't fight city hall" and that the developer was a "townie" who always got his way. But my feeling is you shouldn't get discouraged if you hear statements like that. If you believe in something, you have to stand up for it. Don't ever give up the fight against a poorly sited development, pollution, or anything environmentally dangerous. If you do, you are giving up on the world. Even if you don't win, at least you will have tried.

After nine months and much hard work, the developer, the neighborhood association, the state Department of Environmental Quality Engineering,

2 **selectmen:** elected officials, similar to city councilmen

and others showed up to give the site a deep-hole test to find out if it was suitable for building. The test checks the soil's drainage by seeing if a deeply dug hole will fill with water. I was fairly confident that the site would fail, because I had known that land a long time. But I can tell you that when the test confirmed my beliefs, I was excited and relieved. (Even if the site had passed the test, I would have kept fighting anyway.)

The town of Chelmsford then officially "denied comprehensive permit," a legal step that ensured the development would not be built and that nothing of the same magnitude could ever be constructed there. So the land is safe—for the time being. I'm now trying to get funding from the state to buy the site outright to protect it.

To all of the people who read this article, I challenge you to come to the defense of the environment. It is not just the destruction of the rain forests, the acid rain, and the ozone layer that should concern us, but also our own communities. We can work to stop building developments that are hazardous to life and land. We can recycle plastics, glass, and paper. We can save water and use far less energy than we do.

It is not all that hard to help in the fight to save our planet, Earth. If we are all a little more caring and careful, we will be much closer to saving our environment for ourselves and for future generations. ✍

Animals, Vegetables and Minerals

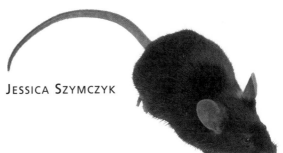

JESSICA SZYMCZYK

I've been a vegetarian (an ovo-lacto vegetarian,[1] to be exact) since I was 13 years old. I don't wear cosmetics. I won't buy or wear fur. I refuse to wear or use leather if at all possible. And I absolutely love animals. I live with fish, a mouse, a pony, a horse and cats, and I'm looking for the perfect dog to complement my other companion animals. Oh, yes. I also love rats. I've had rats for pets. The last was a big black-and-white-hooded rat. I even nursed an abandoned baby mouse, whose eyes had not yet opened, until she reached adulthood.

So why am I working in a biomedical research lab that uses animals in its experiments? No, I am not an infiltrator from the so-called "animal rights" movement. I love what I do, and I get angry when I hear the terrible things animal-rights groups like People for the Ethical Treatment of Animals say about me and my colleagues and how we supposedly treat laboratory animals.

If you buy into the stories of some animal-rightists, I am the last person you would expect to find working at an animal research lab. Well, not only are these groups wrong about me and my profession; they are also grossly mistaken about my colleagues, our work and the conditions under which we keep our animals.

The work we do with animals is crucial. It's important to me as a woman, as a human and as an animal lover. Although most of my work as a veterinary technician involves rodents, two new studies I find pretty

---

1 **ovo-lacto vegetarian:** one who eats only foods from plants, eggs, and milk

exciting involve dogs. In one, my dogs undergo a minor surgical procedure and take one pill a day of a promising drug that may regenerate bone
in victims of osteoarthritis, a condition that cripples many elderly folks. In
the second, we're investigating a drug that stimulates T-cell and white-
blood-cell production, something of vital importance to AIDS patients.

Both would likely be condemned by the rightists as cruel and unnec-
essary. Let me tell you the extent of the "cruelty" my dogs undergo. In
the first study, they play with a lab technician for an hour every day. The
other experiment requires that they drink a tiny amount of an extremely
diluted drug, about a fifth of a teaspoonful, every day for eight days, and
have some blood drawn. When I draw blood, the dogs are happy to see
me and they romp about like bouncy pups. Contrary to popular belief, all
animals are not euthanized[2] at the end of a study. Those that are receive
the same treatment from a veterinarian that your pet would in a veterinary hospital.

How do I justify my profession in view of my beliefs? I want to dispel
any idea that I do what I do for the money. I've wanted to work with animals—horses, actually—since I was old enough to think such thoughts.
My first job out of high school was working for a wonderful and com-
passionate veterinarian for $4 an hour. Until then I had always imagined
myself working on a farm where I could train and ride horses.

I guess you could say my desire to work with animals caused me to go
back to school, where I earned a degree in equine[3] veterinary science
with a minor in animal science. I spent a few years as a vet tech in pri-
vate practice taking care of sick animals, assisting with surgery and
dealing with the pet owners. From that experience I can honestly say at
least 25 percent of pet owners should never be allowed near any animals.
The stories I could tell about pet mistreatment are not fit for any ears.

I'd never considered working in a biomedical lab until a friend invited me
to apply where he worked. I did not know what to expect. TV images of
dark, dirty, water-dripping dungeons floated in and out of my imagination.
I didn't really want to go, but I knew he was a good person and wouldn't be
associated with a bad place, so I applied. The moment I stepped into the lab
was an eye-opener. I was impressed with how clean, well lit and modern
the facilities are. It's more like a human hospital. The monitoring equipment, the sterile technique used in the surgery area, the anesthetics and

2 **euthanized:** mercy-killed
3 **equine:** horse-related

painkillers for postoperative recovery are identical to what you would find in most hospitals for humans.

The animals themselves are frisky, playful and happy to see the animal techs, who play with them whenever they have a free moment. All the dogs have play toys. Do you know of any other hospital where the patient is held in a nurse's arms until he or she awakes and is steady enough to walk alone? That is part of what I do for every animal undergoing anesthesia, whether it's a rat, mouse, cat or a dog.

What impressed me then, and still does now that I am a part of the team, is the absolute honor, respect and devotion all of us have for the animals. Love for the animals is the rule, not the exception. The protective clothing worn by visitors to the lab is to protect the animals.

I take my profession very seriously. And I get angry when I hear people who don't know what they are talking about rant and rave about "torture" and duplication of tests. The research we do is essential to humans and animals. Test duplications are sometimes needed to show that the results of the first study aren't a fluke. Less than 5 percent of our studies require any pain relief at all. A full 95 percent are less painful than a visit to the doctor for you or me.

I've thought about the difference between animal welfare and animal rights. The whole issue of moral and ethical treatment of animals has been one that has shaped how I live my life. But there are some animal-rightists whose definitions and priorities are so extreme that they just don't apply. PETA, I've read, envisions a future where I would not be allowed to keep my pets. And it considers a rat, a mammal, the equal of a child, so deciding to save one or the other would be a flip of a coin. I cannot accept this. My love for animals matches anyone's, but there's no question in my mind as to who would come first.

Biomedical research has become my life. I know how researchers treat lab animals, including mice and rats. I see how the work we are doing truly benefits everyone, including animals. Today, dogs and cats can enjoy a three-to-five-year increase in their life expectancies thanks to research and the vaccines and medicines we've developed. I'm glad to be working with animals and other animal lovers to find ways to make life better for both. ❧

Working against Time

DAVID WAGONER

By the newly bulldozed logging road, for a hundred yards,
I saw the sprawling five-foot hemlocks, their branches crammed
Into each other's light, upended or wrenched aslant
Or broken across waists the size of broomsticks
Or bent, crushed slewfoot[1] on themselves in the duff[2] like briars,[3]
Their roots coming at random out of the dirt, and dying.

I had no burlap in the trunk, not even a spade,
And the shirt off my back wasn't enough to go around.
I'm no tree surgeon, it wasn't Arbor Day, but I climbed
Over the free-for-all, untangling winners and losers
And squeezing as many as I could into my car.
When I started, nothing was singing in the woods except me.

I hardly had room to steer—roots dangled over my shoulder
And scraped the side of my throat as if looking for water.
Branches against the fog on the windshield dabbled designs
Like kids or hung out the vent. The sun was falling down.
It's against the law to dig up trees. Working against
Time and across laws, I drove my ambulance

Forty miles in the dark to the house and began digging
Knee-deep graves for most of them, while the splayed headlights
Along the highway picked me out of the night:
A fool with a shovel searching for worms or treasure
Both buried behind the sweat on his forehead. Two green survivors
Are tangled under the biting rain as I say this.

---

1 **slewfoot:** with twisted feet
2 **duff:** organic debris on the forest floor
3 **briars:** thorns

The King of the Beasts

PHILIP JOSÉ FARMER

The biologist was showing the distinguished visitor through the zoo and laboratory.

"Our budget," he said, "is too limited to re-create all known extinct species. So we bring to life only the higher animals, the beautiful ones that were wantonly exterminated. I'm trying, as it were, to make up for brutality and stupidity. You might say that man struck God in the face every time he wiped out a branch of the animal kingdom."

He paused, and they looked across the moats and the force fields. The quagga[1] wheeled and galloped, delight and sun flashing off his flanks. The sea otter poked his humorous whiskers from the water. The gorilla peered from behind bamboo. Passenger pigeons strutted. A rhinoceros trotted like a dainty battleship. With gentle eyes a giraffe looked at them, then resumed eating leaves.

"There's the dodo. Not beautiful but very droll. And very helpless. Come. I'll show you the re-creation itself."

In the great building, they passed between rows of tall and wide tanks. They could see clearly through the windows and the jelly within.

"Those are African elephant embryos," said the biologist. "We plan to grow a large herd and then release them on the new government preserve."

"You positively radiate," said the distinguished visitor. "You really love the animals, don't you?"

---

1 **quagga:** an extinct animal that was similar to the zebra

"I love all life."

"Tell me," said the visitor, "where do you get the data for re-creation?"

"Mostly, skeletons and skins from the ancient museums. Excavated books and films that we suc-ceeded in restoring and then translating. Ah, see those huge eggs? The chicks of the giant moa[2] are growing within them. These, almost ready to be taken from the tank, are tiger cubs. They'll be dan-gerous when grown but will be confined to the preserve."

The visitor stopped before the last of the tanks.

"Just one?" he said. "What is it?"

"Poor little thing," said the biologist, now sad. "It will be so alone. But I shall give it all the love I have."

"Is it so dangerous?" said the visitor. "Worse than elephants, tigers and bears?"

"I had to get special permission to grow this one," said the biologist. His voice qua-vered.

The visitor stepped sharply back from the tank. He said, "Then it must be. . . . But you wouldn't dare!"

The biologist nod-ded.

"Yes. It's a man." ∾

2 **moa:** an extinct bird that was large and flightless, similar to an ostrich

Responding to Cluster Three

How Can We Live in Harmony with Nature?

Thinking Skill PROBLEM SOLVING

1. "A picture is worth a thousand words," according to one old saying. Imagine that you are the editor of an ecology magazine who is developing an issue focused on any of the ecological problems described so far in this book. Describe the photograph you would put on the cover to draw readers' attention to the problem.

2. In "Animals, Vegetables and Minerals," Jessica Szymczyk tells readers that although animals should be treated with kindness and respect, in matters such as medical research there is no question that humans come first. Explain why you agree or disagree.

3. *Arachnophobia* means "fear of spiders." Why do you think some people are afraid of creatures such as spiders, bats, and snakes?

4. The title of "David Meets Goliath at City Hall" obviously refers to the Biblical story of David and Goliath. In what ways is author Andrew Holleman like David and the land developers like Goliath?

Writing Activity: Future World Scenario

Science fiction writers often create future societies based on one or two simple premises or "what if?" questions. For example, a writer might ask the question, "What would happen if people lost contact with nature because they never went outside?" Or "What would happen if pollution dramatically changed the world's climate?" The writer then uses that premise as the basis of a story.

With a partner, come up with a premise based on one or more environmental issues. Then use that premise to create a scenario or plot outline for a short story.

A Future World Scenario

* presents the premise or "what if?" question.

* shows the impact the problem is having on the world or society.

* outlines a series of events (plot).

* bring matters to a crisis and conclusion.

* often goes on to serve as the basis of a more complete piece of writing, such as a short story or script.

CLUSTER FOUR

Thinking on Your Own

Thinking Skill   SYNTHESIZING

A Young Environmentalist Speaks Out

SEVERN CULLIS-SUZUKI

Hello, I'm Severn Suzuki. . . .

Coming up here today, I have no hidden agenda. I am fighting for my future. Losing my future is not like losing an election or a few points on the stock market. . . .

I am afraid to go out in the sun now because of the holes in the ozone. I am afraid to breathe the air because I don't know what chemicals are in it. I used to go fishing in Vancouver[1] with my dad until just a few years ago we found the fish full of cancers. And now we hear about animals and plants becoming extinct every day—vanishing forever.

In my life, I have dreamed of seeing the great herds of wild animals, jungles and rainforests full of birds and butterflies, but now I wonder if they will even exist for my children to see. Did you have to worry about these little things when you were my age?

All this is happening before our eyes and yet we act as if we have all the time we want and all the solutions. I'm only a child and I don't have all the solutions, but I want you to realize, neither do you!

You don't know how to fix the holes in our ozone layer.

You don't know how to bring salmon back up a dead stream.

You don't know how to bring back an animal now extinct.

1 **Vancouver:** city in the Canadian province of British Columbia

And you can't bring back the forests that once grew where there is now desert.

If you don't know how to fix it, please stop breaking it!

Here you may be delegates of your governments, businesspeople, organizers, reporters, or politicians. But really you are mothers and fathers, sisters and brothers, aunts and uncles. And each of you is somebody's child. . . .

Two days ago here in Brazil, we were shocked when we spent some time with some children living on the streets. . . .

I can't stop thinking that these children are my own age, and that it makes a tremendous difference where you are born. I could be one of those children living in the *favellas*² of Rio. I could be a child starving in Somalia, a victim of war in the Middle East or a beggar in India.

I'm only a child yet I know if all the money spent on *war* was spent on ending poverty and finding environmental answers, what a wonderful place this Earth would be.

At school, even in kindergarten, you teach us to behave in the world. You teach us:

not to fight with others
to work things out
to respect others
to clean up our mess
not to hurt other creatures
to share, not to be greedy.

Then why do you go out and do the things you tell us not to do?

Parents should be able to comfort their children by saying, "Everything's going to be all right"; "We're doing the best we can" and "It's not the end of the world." But I don't think you can say that to us anymore. Are we even on your list of priorities?

My dad always says, "You are what you do, not what you say."

Well, what you do makes me cry at night.

You grown-ups say you love us. I challenge you, *please*, make your actions reflect your words.

Thank you for listening. ∾

---

2 **favellas:** Portuguese for settlements of shacks on the outskirts of a city

The Mushroom

H. M. HOOVER

In A.D. 450 a squirrel could travel from the east coast of North America to the Mississippi without ever leaving the trees.

That year a squirrel, while grooming, brushed several million mushroom spores from its fur.

So small that a hundred million could fit into a teaspoon, the spores floated. Some rose up into the atmosphere; some were carried around the world by the jet stream.[1] Most drifted to the forest floor.

There was a massive, rolling earthquake, followed by electrical storms. Rain fell lightly, steadily, for days.

From two of these spores a new mushroom began to grow. It sent out microscopic filaments,[2] called hyphae, to penetrate and feed on forest debris. A sheath of a thousand hyphae is no thicker than a human hair.

The hyphae secreted enzymes to break down complex carbohydrates into sugars on which the mushroom fed. Needing protein for a balanced diet, the fungi filaments hunted, entrapping and digesting amoebas, bacteria, and tiny worms.

Within months miles of hyphae twisted through the forest floor. The fungi fruited, producing a new mushroom.

A chipmunk and several beetles ate most of the mushroom, scattering spores. Soon a ring-shaped colony of mushrooms marked the spot where the parent once stood.

---

1 **jet stream:** a current of high-speed winds high in the earth's atmosphere
2 **filaments:** very thin threads

In Europe, Attila the Hun[3] died in 453. Tea was brought to China from India.

The ancient forest remained undisturbed. Rains fell and summer nights were warm. Within a few years the mushroom's filaments had spread through an acre and weighed two thousand five hundred pounds.

By the time Arthur, king of the Britons, died in 537, the mushroom had consumed almost a century of fallen trees. Its filaments stretched through ten acres of the forest floor, fruiting in circles the Britons would have called fairy rings.

That year the plague reached northern Europe. A third of the population died. Earthquakes shook the entire world. The Byzantine Empire[4] began to crumble.

The mushroom went on growing.

By 750 the Venerable Bede[5] had written his history of England, newspapers were being printed in China, and some Europeans slept in beds instead of on the floor.

The mushroom's total weight now exceeded eighteen tons, all of it hidden beneath the surface of the forest floor.

By the year 1000, in North America, the Mississippian people lived in handsome cities, but the pueblos[6] of Mesa Verde were running short of water. In the century to come humans sometimes walked over the mushroom's growth. Their moccasins left no footprints.

About that time white men first walked among the tall trees. Fierce as they were, the ancient forest frightened them. It was too big, too dark, too endless. They spent a night in the shelter of a giant hollow oak. When morning came, they hurried back to their Viking ship and fled. They left their fire burning. The tree, mortally wounded, fell in an autumn storm.

The mushroom's hyphae sought out the fallen tree and began to return its mass to the earth and air. Seedlings rooted in the damp, rotting bark.

By 1066 a colonnade[7] of tall trees grew over the giant log, embracing it with their buttress[8] roots. In Europe, Westminster Abbey was consecrated,[9] York Cathedral begun, Edward the Confessor died horribly, his

---

3 **Attila the Hun:** bloodthirsty king of the Huns

4 **Byzantine Empire:** an ancient kingdom in what is now Turkey

5 **Venerable Bede:** a scholar and historian

6 **pueblos:** Indian villages

7 **colonnade:** row, series

8 **buttress:** supporting

9 **consecrated:** dedicated to God

successor was killed in the Battle of Hastings. Then, too, an Italian monk taught his brother monks to sing *do, re, mi,* and the comet later called Halley's appeared. Again.

The comet was as indifferent as the forest and the mushroom to the affairs of humankind.

The Crusades[10] came and went. Saladin[11] terrified all infidels. The Chinese introduced tea to their neighbors, the Japanese. Marco Polo,[12] against his will, was given time to dictate his memoirs. Queens were still the only women noted by historians.

The mushroom's hyphae now spread through more than thirty acres; its mass exceeded thirty-eight tons. It had lived nearly a thousand years

---

10 **Crusades:** series of military expeditions by Christians to win the Holy Land from the Muslims in the eleventh to thirteenth centuries

11 **Saladin:** an eleventh century Muslim warrior

12 **Marco Polo:** an Italian traveler

when Joan of Arc[13] was burned at the stake. The Incas had begun to rule Peru. Lorenzo de' Medici[14] and Christopher Columbus were born. The book-publishing profession began.

In 1592, in Holland, windmills were first used to power mechanical saws.

The day the Pilgrims landed at New Plymouth, the end of the ancient forest became only a matter of time—a long time in human terms, but not for the forest, or the mushroom.

The mushroom's filaments had woven through more than two hundred acres. The weight of its total mass was now as unimaginable as the infinite smallness of the two original spores had once been.

Europeans had no more than landed when they began to cut down trees. Forests that had been evolving for ten thousand years into perfect ecosystems disappeared in two centuries.

The mushroom's home, far from the coast, survived longer than most. Inexorably the settlers came, cutting, burning, blasting, plowing around the stumps.

In the winter of 1866 the mushroom's forest was cut, the wood sold to the Union army.[15] The frozen soil saved the mushroom from destruction. Seedlings sprouted in the sunlight of the following spring. Deer grazed among the fairy rings.

In 1904 a German couple bought the land where the mushroom grew. Father and sons slowly cleared the trees and plowed, and replowed. Only forty acres were spared as "woods."

In 1984 the family farm was sold to a developer. Bulldozers arrived. A shopping mall was built over the rich fields. A parking lot covered the acres that had long been forest. Sun on the black asphalt superheated the earth below.

The week before the mall's opening, rain fell softly, steadily, for days. One night a bulge appeared on the surface of the parking lot, and another and another. Soon there were too many to count, and they formed circular patterns.

---

13 **Joan of Arc:** a French peasant girl who became a hero by leading the army into victory over the English in 1429; later she was burned at the stake as a witch by the English

14 **Lorenzo de' Medici:** an Italian statesman whose leadership helped make Florence one of the world's most beautiful cities

15 **Union army:** the Northern army in the American Civil War

Had you been there, you might have heard above the rain the rasp of breaking asphalt, the slow cracking of masonry walls, cascades of breaking glass.

Morning light revealed that the mall and parking lot had been lifted and were being held aloft atop the caps of millions of mushrooms . . . fairy rings.

As the mushrooms aged, the buildings standing on them swayed and sagged. Girders detached, roofs fell in, walls collapsed. In the parking lot the light poles stood at crazy angles, creaking in the wind that blew across a field of broken asphalt.

By noon the mushrooms had released trillions of spores to the wind. Some spores rose into the atmosphere to travel with the jet stream. Others drifted into the wreckage or were washed into raw earth.

New mushrooms began to grow. They sent out microscopic filaments to penetrate and feed upon the debris. A sheath of a thousand hyphae is no thicker than a human hair. ∾

Duck Hunting

Gary Paulsen

After grouse, after rabbits, after bow hunting for deer, but before the long winter hunts, there was duck hunting.

Sometimes it was walking along the river out of town, starting in the cold mornings, the rainy cold mornings of late October when nobody sane went outside.

Teal flew along the river, their wings whistling, and were difficult to hit because they flew so fast and never seemed to reveal themselves until it was too late to raise the old single-barrel sixteen-gauge[1] and shoot.

Jump-shooting[2] mallards was better. Wayne had a smokey-black Lab[3] named Ike after the president, and he would retrieve with a lily-soft mouth no matter who shot the duck. North of town there were chains of swamps with open, small potholes of dark water where the mallards would sit. It was hard to walk because the peat under the swamp-grass was unfrozen and springy and frequently allowed a foot to go through down into the mud, where it tried to suck a boot off. But a rhythm could be felt after a time, and it was possible to move forward. Because the grass was so deep the mallards would be surprised, and it was while they were rising, their wings pounding to give them altitude—it was then that sometimes a shot could be taken, and Ike would watch with even brown

---

1 **single-barrel sixteen-gauge:** shotgun with one discharging tube that is slightly smaller in diameter than the twelve-gauge commonly used in hunting

2 **jump-shooting:** a technique in which hunters sneak up on birds in water and flush them into the air

3 **Lab:** short for Labrador retriever, a breed of dog often used for bringing back, or retrieving, game

eyes for the mallard to fall. At the moment it was hit, when it went from the beauty of a flying duck to the broken form of death—at that moment Ike would leap forward into the pothole and sometimes be waiting when the duck hit the water.

But there was an uncle . . .

Walk-hunting was fine except that it was limited and so clumsy that some of the art was lost.

But there was an uncle who had a duck-boat and an old truck and a rusty brown Chesapeake retriever[4] named Robby, and the uncle and Robby took the boy out one morning to hunt ducks, and though the boy never hunted that way again it was in him and his mind from then on.

The uncle had just come back from fighting in Korea[5] and would be in the boy's life for only one year before the uncle would move on to Montana, where he would hole up and think on what he had done and seen in Korea.

He loved the dog and took it with him everywhere, talked to it as if it were a person, and sometimes would even read to the dog out of books he carried that had strange-sounding names the boy could not under-stand, though there were several of them on the dashboard of the truck and the boy could read the titles on the spine. Titles like *The Collected Writings of Plato* and *Aristotelian Thinking*.

The boy did not sleep the whole night before and was up waiting when the uncle arrived at four o'clock.

It was pitch-dark and cold—so cold there was ice on the puddles left by rain during the night. The truck was a 1940 Ford with a cranky heater, but Robby was in the front seat with the uncle and climbed on the boy as soon as he got in the truck. The dog was warm and smelled of dog food and outside, and the boy cuddled with him while they drove north out of town to the flat swampy lakes that sat squat in the middle of the main migratory flight path.[6]

At some point on the drive in the old truck through the dark morning the boy fell asleep with his face buried in the dog's neck-fur. He was awakened by the sound of the uncle talking.

"We'll work that stand of rice on the south end of the lake."

The voice was soft, even.

4 **Chesapeake retriever:** short for Chesapeake Bay retriever, a breed of sporting dog

5 **fighting in Korea:** the war between North and South Korea in the early fifties. The U.S sent troops to help South Korea.

6 **migratory flight path:** the route birds take when travelling to and from different climates

"Come in there quiet, before first light, and try to catch the early-dawn movers like we did last time. . . ."

The boy nodded, but he felt the dog move and cock his ears and lean away and realized the uncle was talking to the dog and not him.

"May be some geese moving, too," the uncle said. "Most of them are already gone south but there might be a few." The uncle poured hot coffee from a thermos expertly, while driving, popped the cork back in the mouth of the thermos and then produced a half pint of Calvert Reserve from his duck-coat pocket and dropped a generous amount in the hot coffee. The smell of the whiskey on top of the hot coffee immediately filled the cab of the truck, but the boy pretended not to notice because he did not like drinking. To hide the smell of the whiskey he buried his nose in the dog's fur again.

The uncle spoke no more but sipped the coffee in silence while they drove for another half hour. Then he turned off the main road and killed the headlights and drove for ten or fifteen minutes in darkness so black the boy could see only a dim bulk of trees to the side of the track.

The dog knew where they were and became excited when the uncle stopped the truck.

Without speaking he climbed out of the truck and moved around to the rear. He pulled rubber boots out of the back end and jerked them on over his regular boots, then waited while the boy—who was already wearing rubber boots because that's all he had—came around the truck to help with the duck-boat.

The boat was twelve feet long, flat on the bottom and pointed at both ends so it would slide through the swamp-grass more easily. In the center was a seven-foot-long cockpit where two men and a dog could sit if they remained still and patient.

They put the boat in the water—or rather the uncle guided the boat, because it was still so dark he could see nothing—and the dog jumped in without having to be told.

The uncle brought two guns and handed the boy one—a sixteen-gauge Ithaca pump[7] as old or older than he was—and put boxes of shells in the boat.

"Get in."

The boy was so excited that he tripped and stumbled and would have fallen had the uncle not caught him and helped him.

7 **Ithaca pump:** Ithaca is a brand. A pump gun ejects a fired shell while pumping the next shell into the chamber, ready to be fired.

The boy moved to the front of the boat, and the uncle climbed in the back and laid his shotgun down and a large gunnysack down, stood and worked the pole with the steel expanding feet against the grass to propel the boat through the weeds and stands of rice.

It was still dark, but now the boy could see outlines, edges, and he watched ahead of the boat and made out the shape of a blind just before the boat bumped into it. The uncle poled back, moved the nose over, and worked slowly to the front of the blind. When the boat was in a small patch of clear water, he opened the sack and pulled out decoys,[8] arranged them in a kind of fan, each held down with a lead sinker and a cord. Then he turned the boat and slid it back inside the blind, where he squatted down and laid the pole to the side on the grass.

"We'd better load—the light will come fast now when it comes."

He flipped his shotgun over, and the boy did the same with the Ithaca pump, loaded it with three high-base shells from the box on the floor of the boat and studied the weapon in the new morning light.

The boy had never seen such a gun. All the bluing[9] was worn, but it had been kept in perfect shape and coated with a light film of fine oil that jumped to his fingers and somehow to his mouth and he could taste the steel, taste the bluing, taste all the hunts the gun had been on, taste the years of the gun.

He loaded it, and when he worked the pump to chamber a shell the action was so worn it almost worked itself, closed with a soft "snicking" sound that made him shiver and expect something he did not understand—some great adventure.

When the ducks came, the first ducks, they were high, just spots in the barely lighted sky, and the uncle used a call to make the mallard feeding chuckle, and for a moment nothing happened. Then a small flock of eight or ten ducks set their wings and broke off in a long glide down toward the blind.

The boy could not stand it and when the ducks were still well out of range he rose and fired, wobbling the boat and startling both the uncle and the dog.

The ducks veered away and the sudden explosion brought up hundreds of them that had been in the weeds around the boat. The boy stared, open-mouthed, while the uncle fired from a sitting position; once, twice, and two of the jumpers fell.

8 **decoys:** artificial birds used by hunters to lure live birds into shooting range

9 **bluing:** a protective blue-black coating used to finish a gun and protect it from rusting

Before they hit the weeds Robby was over the side and heading for them. He brought one back within a minute—while the boy still stared—and went back for the other without being told. This one he found after working the weeds with his head down, belly-deep in swampwater, and carried it back with a wing flapping because the duck was still alive. The uncle quickly killed it and then turned to the boy and said, simply, "Maybe next time will be better."

And the next time was better.

A flock came in again high, specks in the gray-dawn sky, and the uncle called again, used the soft low chuckling sound from the call, and once more a group broke from the flock and started the glide down.

"I'll shoot left," the uncle whispered. "You right."

It was almost impossible to wait. The ducks seemed to hang in the air, caught on currents of wind that wouldn't let them down.

But they came, floating in a curve well out to the side to give them approach and landing room, and it seemed they would hit the water any second.

But this time the boy waited, watching the uncle out of the corner of his eye, waited until he couldn't stand it, and then waited even more until it seemed the ducks were going to land, were on their final approach, barely skimming the water near the decoys, and at last the uncle raised his shotgun and the boy did too and aimed at the duck on the right, aimed just in front of him and pulled the trigger.

Two ducks fell. The uncle had fired at exactly the same moment. The boy heard the pump work on the uncle's gun, did the same with his, and aimed at a mallard working to get high, flying straight up away from the water, and the boy fired and saw the duck break.

That's how it looked. How he thought of it. The duck broke. Its wings etched against the sky, broken and falling, the neck curved over back-wards and he thought then, could not help but think then of the doe, the way the doe looked when she lay down in the grass and put her head over and down, and he had the first moment of true doubt; doubt that would plague him the rest of his life, moral doubt, growing doubt, doubt that ended childhood and in some measure ended the joy of hunting just as he had ended the duck and the doe.

Doubt that, ultimately, took him from the woods and the damp-smelling Chesapeake dog sitting in the gray morning, out into the real world, which he learned to live in but never learned to love as he had the world of hunting and fishing as a boy. ∽

The Last Dog

KATHERINE PATERSON

Brock approached the customs gate.[1] Although he did not reach for the scanner, a feeling, it might have been labeled "excitement," made him tremble. His fingers shook as he punched in his number on the inquiry board. "This is highly irregular, Brock 095670038," the disembodied voice said. "What is your reason for external travel?"

Brock took a deep breath. "Scientific research," he replied. He didn't need to be told that his behavior was "irregular." He'd never heard of anyone doing research outside the dome—actual rather than virtual research. "I—I've been cleared by my podmaster and the Research Team. . . ."

"Estimated time of return?" So, he wasn't to be questioned further.

"Uh, 1800 hours."

"Are you wearing the prescribed dry suit with helmet and gloves?"

"Affirmative."

"You should be equipped with seven hundred fifty milliliters of liquid and food tablets for one day travel."

"Affirmative." Brock patted the sides of the dry suit to be sure.

"Remember to drink sparingly. Water supply is limited." Brock nodded. He tried to lick his parched lips, but his whole mouth felt dry. "Is that understood?"

"Affirmative." Was he hoping customs would stop him? If he was, they didn't seem to be helping him. Well, this was what he wanted, wasn't it?

---

1 **customs gate:** the place where travelers must stop and have goods they are bringing in or out of a country approved and sometimes taxed

To go outside the dome.

"Turn on the universal locator, Brock 095670038, and proceed to gate."

Why weren't they questioning him further? Were they eager for him to go? Ever since he'd said out loud in group speak that he wanted to go outside the dome, people had treated him strangely—that session with the podmaster and then the interview with the representative from Research. Did they think he was a deviant? Deviants sometimes disappeared. The word was passed around that they had "gone outside," but no one really knew. No deviant had ever returned.

The gate slid open. Before he was quite ready for it, Brock found himself outside the protection of the dome. He blinked. The sun—at least it was what was called "the sun" in virtual lessons—was too bright for his eyes even inside the tinted helmet. He took a deep breath, one last backward look at the dome, which, with the alien sun gleaming on it, was even harder to look at than the distant star, and started across an expanse of brown soil [was it?] to what he recognized from holograms[2] as a line of purplish mountains in the distance.

It was, he pulled the scanner from his outside pouch and checked it, "hot." Oh, that was what he was feeling. Hot. He remembered "hot" from a virtual lesson he'd had once on deserts. He wanted to take off the dry suit, but he had been told since he could remember that naked skin would suffer irreparable burning outside the protection of the dome. He adjusted the control as he walked so that the unfamiliar perspiration would evaporate. He fumbled a bit before he found the temperature adjustment function. He put it on twenty degrees centigrade and immediately felt more comfortable. No one he really knew had ever left the dome, (stories of deviants exiting the dome being hard to verify), but there was all this equipment in case someone decided to venture out. He tried to ask the clerk who outfitted him, but the woman was evasive. The equipment was old, she said. People used to go out, but the outside environment was threatening, so hardly anyone (she looked at him carefully now), hardly anyone ever used it now.

Was Brock, then, the only normal person still curious about the outside? Or had all those who had dared to venture out perished, discouraging further forays? Perhaps he was a deviant for wanting to see the mountains for himself. When he'd mentioned it to others, they had laughed, but there was a hollow sound to the laughter.

---

2 **holograms:** three-dimensional images that appear real but aren't; generally produced by lasers

If he never returned, he'd have no one to blame but himself. He knew that. While his podfellows played virtual games, he'd wandered into a subsection of the historical virtuals called "ancient fictions." Things happened in these fictions more—well, more densely than they did in the virtuals. The people he met there—it was hard to describe—but somehow they were more *actual* than dome dwellers. They had strange names like Huck Finn and M. C. Higgins the Great. They were even a little scary. It was their insides. Their insides were very loud. But even though the people in the ancient fictions frightened him a bit, he couldn't get enough of them. When no one was paying attention, he went back again and again to visit them. They had made him wonder about that other world—that world outside the dome.

Perhaps, once he had realized the danger the ancient fictions posed, he should have left them alone, but he couldn't help himself. They had made him feel hollow, hungry for something no food pellet or even virtual experience could satisfy. And now he was in that world they spoke of and the mountains of it were in plain view.

He headed for the purple curves. Within a short distance from the dome, the land was clear and barren, but after he had been walking for an hour or so he began to pass rusting hulks and occasional ruins of what might have been the dwellings of ancient peoples that no one in later years had cleared away for recycling or vaporization.

He checked the emotional scanner for an unfamiliar sensation. "Loneliness," it registered. He rather liked having names for these new sensations. It made him feel a bit "proud," was it? The scanner was rather interesting. He wondered when people had stopped using them. He hadn't known they existed until, in that pod meeting, he had voiced his desire to go outside.

The podmaster had looked at him with a raised eyebrow and a sniff. "Next thing you'll be asking for a scanner," he said.

"What's a scanner?" Brock asked.

The podmaster requisitioned one from storage, but at the same time, he must have alerted Research, because it was the representative from Research who had brought him the scanner and questioned him about his expressed desire for an Actual Adventure—a journey outside the dome.

"What has prompted this, uh—unusual ambition?" the representative had asked, his eyes not on Brock but on the scanner in his hand. Brock had hesitated, distracted by the man's fidgeting with the strange instrument. "I—I'm interested in scientific research," Brock said at last.

So here he was out of the pod, alone for the first time in his life. Perhaps, though, he should have asked one of his podfellows to come along. Or even the pod robopet. But the other fellows all laughed when he spoke of going outside, their eyes darting back and forth. Nothing on the outside, they said, could equal the newest Virtual Adventure. He suddenly realized that ever since he started interfacing with the ancient fictions, his fellows had given him that look. They did think he was odd—not quite the same as a regular podfellow. Brock didn't really vibe with the pod robopet. It was one of the more modern ones, and when they'd programmed its artificial intelligence they'd somehow made it too smart. The robopet in the children's pod last year was older, stupider, and more "fun" to have around.

He'd badly underestimated the distance to the mountains. The time was well past noon, and he had at least three kilometers to go. Should he signal late return or turn about now? He didn't have much more than one day's scant supply of water and food tablets. But he was closer to the hills than to the dome. He felt a thrill ["excitement"] and he pressed on.

There were actual trees growing on the first hill. Not the great giants of virtual history lessons, more scrubby and bent. But they were trees, he was sure of it. The podmaster had said that trees had been extinct for hundreds of years. Brock reached up and pulled off a leaf. It was green and had veins. In some ways it looked like his own hand. He put the leaf in his pack to study later. He didn't want anyone accusing him of losing his scientific objectivity. Only deviants did that. Farther up the hill he heard an unfamiliar burbling sound. No, he knew that sound. It was water running. He'd heard it once when the liquid dispenser had malfunctioned. There'd been a near panic in the dome over it. He checked the scanner. There was no caution signal, so he hurried toward the sound.

It was a—a "brook"—he was sure of it! Virtual lessons had taught that there were such things outside in the past but that they had long ago grown poisonous, then in the warming climate had dried up. But here was a running brook, not even a four-hour journey from his dome. His first impulse was to take off his protective glove and dip a finger in it, but he drew back. He had been well conditioned to avoid danger. He sat down clumsily on the bank. Yes, this must be grass. There were even some tiny flowers mixed in the grass. Would the atmosphere poison him if he unscrewed his helmet to take a sniff? He punched the scanner to read conditions, but the characters on the scanner panel danced about uncertainly until, at length, the disembodied voice said "conditions unreadable." He'd better not risk it.

He pushed the buttons now for liquid and pellets. A tube appeared in his mouth. It dropped a pellet on his tongue. From the tube he sucked liquid enough to swallow his meal. What was it they called outside nourishment in the history virtuals? *Pecnec?* Something like that. He was having a *pecnec* in the *woods* by a *brook*. A hasty consulting of the scanner revealed that what he was feeling was "pleasure." He was very glad he hadn't come with an anxious podfellow or, worse, an advanced robopet that would, no doubt, be yanking at his suit already, urging him back toward the dome.

It was then, in the middle of post-*pecnec* satisfaction, that he heard the new sound. Like that programmed into a robopet, yet different. He struggled to his feet. The dry suit from storage was certainly awkward when you wanted to stand up or sit down. Nothing on the scanner indicated danger, so he went into the scrubby woods toward the sound. And stopped abruptly.

Something was lying under the shadow of a tree. Something about a meter long. It was furred and quite still. The sound was not coming from it. And then he saw the small dog—the puppy. He was sure it was a puppy, nosing the stiff body of what must once have been its mother, making the little crying sounds that he'd heard from the brook. Later, much later, he realized that he should have been wary. If the older dog had died of some extradomal disease, the puppy might have been a carrier. But at the time, all he could think of was the puppy, a small creature who had lost its mother.

He'd found out about mothers from the Virtuals. Mothers were extinct in the dome. Children were conceived and born in the lab and raised in units of twelve in the pods, presided over by a bank of computers and the podmaster. Nuclear families, as everyone knew, had been wasteful of time, energy, and space. There was an old proverb: The key to survival is efficiency. So though Brock could guess the puppy was "sad" (like that fictions person, Jo, whose podmate expired), he didn't know what missing a mother would feel like. And who would whimper for a test tube?

Brock had never seen a dog, of course, but he had seen plenty of dog breed descriptions on the science/history virtuals. Dogs had been abundant once. They filled the ancient fictions. They even had names there—Lassie, Toto, Sounder. But now dogs were extinct, gone during the dark ages when the atmosphere had become warm and poisonous. The savages who had not had the intelligence or wealth to join the foresighted dome crafters had killed all animals wild or domesticated for

food before they had eventually died out themselves. It was all in one of the very first virtual lessons. He had seen that one many times. He never confessed to anyone how, well, sad it made him feel.

But obviously, dogs were not quite extinct. Cautiously, he moved toward the small one.

"Alert. Alert. Scanning unknown object."

Brock pushed the off button. "Are you sure you want to turn off scanner?"

"Affirmative." He stuck the scanner into his pouch.

The puppy had lifted its head at the sound of his voice. It looked at him, head cocked, as though deciding whether to run or stay.

"It's all right, dog," Brock said soothingly. "I won't hurt you." He stayed still. He didn't want to frighten the little beast. If it ran, he wasn't sure he'd be able to catch it in his clumsy dry suit.

Slowly he extended his gloved hand. The dog backed away anxiously, but when Brock kept the hand extended, the puppy slowly crept toward him and sniffed, making whimpering sounds. It wasn't old enough to be truly afraid, it seemed. The pup licked his glove tentatively, then backed away again. It was looking for food, and plasticine gloves weren't going to satisfy.

Brock looked first at the dead mother whose source of nourishment must have long dried up, then around the landscape. What would a dog eat? A puppy on its own? He took off his glove and reached through his pouch into the inside pocket that held his pellet supply. Making every move slow and deliberate so as not to startle the dog, he held out a pellet. The dog came to his hand, licked it, then the pellet. It wrinkled its nose. Brock laughed. He didn't need the scanner now to tell him that what he felt was "pleasure." He loved the feel of the rough tongue on his palm and the little furred face, questioning him.

"It's all right, fellow. You can eat it."

As though understanding, the pup gulped down the pellet. Then looked around for more, not realizing that it had just bolted down a whole meal. When the dog saw there was no more coming, it ran over to the brook. Brock watched in horror as it put its head right down into the poisonous stream and lapped noisily.

"Don't!" Brock cried.

The puppy turned momentarily at the sound, then went back to drinking, as though it was the most normal thing in the world. Well, it was, for the dog. Where else would a creature in the wild get liquid? If the streams were not all dried up, they must have learned to tolerate the water. But then, it was breathing the poisoned atmosphere, wasn't it? Why hadn't it hit Brock before? This was a fully organic creature on the outside without any life support system. What could that mean? Some amazing mutation must have occurred, making it possible for at least some creatures to breathe the outside atmosphere and drink its poisoned water. Those who couldn't died, those who could survived and got stronger. Even the ancient scientist Darwin knew that. And Brock had come upon one of these magnificent mutants!

The puppy whimpered and looked up at Brock with large, trusting eyes. How could he think of it as a mutant specimen? It was a puppy. One who had lost its mother. What would it eat? There was no sign of food for a carnivore. Perhaps way back in the mountains some small mammals had also survived, keeping the food chain going, but the puppy would not live long enough to find its way there, much less know how to hunt with its mother gone. For the first time in his life something deep inside Brock reached out toward another creature. The thought of the puppy languishing here by the side of its dead parent until it, too . . .

"Your name is Brog, all right?" The ancient astronomers had named stars after themselves. He had discovered something just as wonderful. Didn't he have the right to name it sort of after himself while preserving the puppy's uniqueness? "Don't worry, Brog. I won't let you starve."

Which is why Brock appeared at the customs portal after dark, the front of his dry suit stained, carrying a wriggling Canis familiaris of uncertain breed.

If there had been any way to smuggle the dog in, Brock would have. But he couldn't for the life of him figure out how. As it was, every alarm in the area went off when he stepped into the transitional cubicle. The disembodied voice of the monitor queried him:

"Welcome back, Brock 095670038. You're late."

"Affirmative."

"And you are carrying contraband."

"I pulled a leaf."

"Deposit same in quarantine bins."

"Affirmative."

"Sensors denote warm-blooded presence not on official roster."

"I found a dog," Brock mumbled.

"Repeat."

"A dog."

"Canis familiaris is extinct."

"Well, maybe it's just a robopet that got out somehow."

"Correction. Robopets are bloodless. Leave dry suit for sterilization and proceed to quarantine inspection."

The officials in quarantine inspection, who rarely had anything to inspect, were at first nervous and then, as they watched the puppy happily licking Brock's face, interested despite themselves. An actual dog! None of them had ever seen one, of course, and Brock's dog was so much, well, more vital than a robopet. And although, on later reflection, they knew they should have terminated or expelled it, they couldn't quite bring themselves to do so that night.

"It will have to go to Research," the chief inspector finally declared.

"Permission requested to hand carry the dog known as Brog to Research," Brock said. There was a bit of an argument about that. Several inspectors sought the honor, but the chief declared that Brock, having shed his dry suit and being already contaminated, should be placed with the dog in a hermetically sealed air car and transported to Research.

The scientists in Research were predictably amazed to see a live Canis familiaris. But being scientists and more objective than the lower-grade quarantine inspectors, they kept a safe distance both physically and psychically from the creature. Only the oldest scientist, dressed in proper protective clothing, came into the laboratory with Brock and the dog. He scanned and poked and prodded the poor little fellow until it began to whimper in protest.

"Brog needs to rest," said Brock, interrupting the scientist in the midst of his inspection. "She's (for by this time gender had been indisputably established) had a hard day. And if there's some actual food available—she's not used to pellets."

"Of course, of course," said one of the researchers through the speaker in the observation booth. "How thoughtless. Send someone out for a McLike burger without sauce. She may regard it as meat. Anyhow, it will seem more like food to her than a pellet, affirmative, Brock?"

The scientists, Brock soon realized, were looking to him for advice. He was, after all, the discoverer of the last dog. It gave him sudden scientific status. Brock had sense enough to take advantage of this. After Brog had swallowed the McLike burger in three quick gulps, Brock insisted that he be allowed to stay with Brog, so that he might interact and sleep with her. "She's not like us," he explained. "She's used to tumbling about and curling up with other warm bodies. In the old myths," he added, "puppies separated from their litters cried all night long. She will need constant interaction with another warm-blooded creature or she might well die of," he loved using his new vocabulary, "'loneliness.'"

The scientists agreed. After all, research was rather like quarantine, and since Brock had touched the dog ungloved and unprotected, he might well have picked up some germ from her. It was better to keep them both isolated in the research lab where proper precautions would be taken.

For nearly a week, Brock lived with Brog in the research center, eating McLike burgers, playing "fetch," teaching Brog to "sit," "heel," "come"— all the commands he could cull from the ancient texts. The dog quickly learned to obey Brock's commands, but it wasn't the automatic response of a robopet. Brog delighted in obedience. She wanted to please Brock, and those few times when she was too busy nosing about the lab and failed to obey instantly, those times when Brock's voice took on a sharp tone of reproof, the poor little thing put her tail between her legs, looked up at him with sorrowful eyes, begging to be forgiven. Brock was tempted to speak sharply to her even when there was no need, for the sight of her drooping ears and tail, her mournful eyes was so dear to him that he did what Travis Coates had done to Old Yeller. He hugged her. There was no other way to explain it. He simply put his arms around her and held her to his chest while she beat at him with her tail and licked his face raw. Out of the corner of his eye he was well aware that one of the scientists was watching. Well, let him watch. Nothing was as wonderful as feeling this warmth toward another creature.

For the first week, the researchers seemed quite content to observe dog and boy from their glass-paneled observation booth and speak copious notes into their computers. Only the oldest of them would come into the lab and actually touch the alien creature, and he always wore a sterile protective suit with gloves. The others claimed it would interfere with objectivity if they got close to the dog, but they all seemed to behave positively toward Brog. No mention was made to Brock of his own less than objective behavior. So Brock was astounded to awake in the middle of the night to the sounds of an argument. Someone had forgotten to turn off the communication system.

"Cloning—it's the only thing to do. If she's the last, we owe it to posterity to keep the line going."

"And how are we going to raise a pack of dogs in a dome? One is nearly eating and drinking us out of test tube and petri dish. We can't go on this way. As drastic as it may seem, we have to be realistic. Besides, no one has had the chance to do actual experiments since the dark ages. Haven't you ever, just once, yearned to compare virtual research with actual?"

"What about the boy? He won't agree. Interfacing daily with the dog, he's become crippled by primal urges."

"Can you think what chaos might ensue if a flood of primordial emotions were to surface in a controlled environment such as ours?" another asked. "Apparently, emotions are easily triggered by interactions with primitive beasts, like dogs."

"Shh. Not now. The speaker is—" The system clicked off.

But Brock had already heard. He knew he had lost anything resembling scientific objectivity. He was no longer sure objectivity was a desirable trait. He rather enjoyed being flooded by "primordial emotions." But he was more worried for Brog than for himself. It wasn't hard to figure out what the scientists meant by "actual experiments." Cloning would be bad enough. Ten dogs who looked just like Brog so no one would know how special, how truly unique Brog was. But experiments! They'd cut her open and examine her internal organs, the way scientists had in the dark ages. They'd prod her with electric impulses and put chips in her brain. They'd try to change her personality or modify her behavior. They'd certainly try to make her eat and drink less!

In the dark, he put his arm around Brog and drew her close. He loved the terrible smell of her breath and the way she snored when she slept. They'd probably fix that, too.

The next day he played sick. Brog, faithful dog that she was, hung around him whimpering, licking his face. The scientists showed no particular concern. They were too busy plotting what they might do with Brog.

Brock crept to the nearest terminal in the lab. It was already logged in. The scientists had been doing nothing but research on Canis familiaris. COMMON CANINE DISEASES. Brock scrolled down the list with descriptions. No, distemper wouldn't do. The first symptom was loss of appetite. He couldn't make Brog fake that. On and on it went—no, heartworms wouldn't do. What he needed was a disease that might affect Homo sapiens as well as Canis familiaris. Here it was! Rabies: A viral disease occurring in animals and humans, esp. in dogs and wolves. Transmitted by bite or scratch. The early stages of the disease are most dangerous, for an otherwise healthy and friendly appearing animal will suddenly bite without provocation.

Rabies was it! Somehow he would have to make Brog bite him. There was no antirabies serum in the dome, he felt sure. There were no animals in the dome. Why would they use precious space to store an unneeded medication? So they'd have to expel him as well as Brog for fear of spreading the disease. He shivered, then shook himself. No matter what lay on the outside, he could not stand to go back to the life he had lived in the dome before he met Brog.

He crept back to bed, pulling the covers over Brog. When one of the scientists came into the observation booth, Brock pinched Brog's neck as hard as he could. Nothing. He pinched again, harder. Brog just snuggled closer, slobbering on his arm.

Disgusted, Brock got out of bed. Brog hopped down as well, rubbing against his leg. Pinching obviously was not going to do it. While the scientist on duty in the booth was bending over a computer terminal, Brock brought his foot down on Brog's paw. A tiny yip was all he got from that cruel effort—not enough sound even to make the man look up.

"Feeling better, Brock 095670038?" The oldest researcher had come into the lab.

"Affirmative," Brock answered.

"And how are you, puppy-wuppy?" The old man tickled Brog under her chin with his gloved hand. If I were a dog, I'd bite someone like that, thought Brock, but Brog, of course, simply licked the researcher's glove and wagged her tail.

That was when he got his great idea. He waited to execute it until the proper moment. For the first time, all the scientists had gathered in the lab, all of them in protective garb, some of them twitching nervously in their chairs. They were sitting in a circle around Brock and Brog, explaining what must be done.

"It has to be done for the sake of science," they began. Then they went on to, "For the sake of the dome community, which is always, as you well know, short on food, and particularly short on water." Brock listened to their arguments, nodding solemnly, pretending to agree. "It won't be as if she'll really be gone, you know. We've made virtuals of her—a special series just for you to keep. You can virtually play with her whenever you like."

That was the cue. Brock turned and bit Brog on the tail so hard that the blood started. Brog, surprised and enraged, spun around and bit Brock on the nose.

There was a shocked silence. Every scientist leaned backward, body pressed hard against his or her chair back. Every eye was on the two of them.

"I—I don't know what got into me," Brock said. "I've been feeling very weird." The scientists continued to stare. "I was checking the historical records. . . ."

All of the scientists fled the room. Someone ran to a computer terminal. When Brock offered to take Brog out of the dome and let her loose in the mountains, no one argued. Neither did they say, "Hurry back," or even, "Take care." No one came close as he loaded his pouch with water and food pellets. The customs gate monitor asked no questions.

Out of sight of the dome, Brog was delirious with joy, jumping and running about in circles around Brock's boots. Why wasn't the atmosphere choking Brog if it was as poisonous as the dome dwellers claimed? His heart beating rapidly, Brock unscrewed his helmet just enough to let in a little of the outside atmosphere. Nothing happened. In fact, he seemed to be breathing perfectly normally. He took off the helmet entirely. He was still breathing freely. But his heart was beating so hard, he couldn't be sure. He waited for the choking sensation he had been warned of. It didn't occur. Could they be wrong? Could the outside world have healed itself? Perhaps—perhaps the reason the scanner had so much trouble reading the outside atmosphere was because it wasn't within the range of computerized expectations.

Could it be? Could it be that fear had kept the dome dwellers prisoner many years longer than a poisoned environment would have?

He unfastened the dry suit and slowly stepped out of it into the sunlight.

It was wonderful how much faster he could walk without the clumsy suit. "Who knows?" Brock said to a frisking Brog. "Who knows, maybe out here you aren't the last dog. Your mother had to come from somewhere."

Brog barked happily in reply.

"And maybe, just maybe, where there are dogs, there are humans as well."

They stopped at the brook where they'd met, and both of them had a long drink. Brock no longer carried a scanner, but he knew what he felt was excitement. The water was delicious. ∞

Is the Weather Getting Worse?

Colin Marquis and Stu Ostro

Just last month, a heat wave sent temperatures soaring into triple digits throughout the mid-Atlantic and Northeast, causing half a million people to lose power and killing at least two dozen. Before the month was finished, a second scorcher smothered the Midwest and other parts of the country, this time killing more than 185 in the deadliest heat wave there since 1995. And still yet in July, severe thunderstorms dropped golf ball-sized hail and dumped 13 inches of rain in Iowa, washing out bridges and railroad tracks, closing dozens of roads and whisking an elderly man out of his car. Now, we're in the heart of hurricane season.

The weather is awesome, frightening and spellbinding. It is a rollicking ride with no guarantee of safe return. But are we entering a unique era in weather history? Or are these events "business as usual" for Mother Nature?

As meteorologists with the Weather Channel, we've discovered that the truth may come as a surprise to you: Some of today's weather is wilder, and you can attribute part of that to nature. But blame perception and mankind's actions as well.

Before, tornadoes ripped through Midwest towns, but consequences seemed more distant. Today, real-time multimedia communication means gripping images get beamed instantly from tornado alley into our living rooms—or PCs. It's as if we're all experiencing the bad weather, albeit vicariously. Furthermore, as the population continues to grow, more people and buildings get in the way of whipping winds and flooding waters.

So what's wilder out there: Our perceptions and behaviors? Or the weather itself? Here's our take on what's really happening.

IS IT GETTING HOTTER? YES.

But not as much as you'd think. The Earth has warmed about 1 degree Fahrenheit this century. We all have been inundated with long expositions on human-induced global warming, some of them objective, others not. Inevitably, talk of global warming increases during and just following extreme heat waves such as this past July's. Weather is characterized by ups and downs, activity and monotony. Extremes will always occur, and they do not necessarily foretell of more ominous times to come. Globally, 1998 was the warmest year on record, based on actual measurements as well as satellite data. Still, it is important to remember that specific temperature records over land date back only about 120 years, and data over the oceans (70% of the globe) was quite sparse until about 25 years ago, when satellites became more versatile. Therefore, precise measurements of temperature do not extend far into the past, a mere drop in the bucket when considering the realm of global climate change.

IS IT GETTING WETTER? YES.

Tom Karl at the National Climatic Data Center has found that much of the middle and upper latitudes of the earth—most of the U.S., Canada and Europe—show increases up to 20% this century. Most of that is due to an increase in very heavy precipitation events. As global temperatures increase, one theory goes, more water evaporates from the oceans. The increase in water vapor results in heavier precipitation.

But, again, mankind's development is often its own enemy. As humans continue to develop land, laying concrete and asphalt along the way, it follows that water runoff problems would increase. Even with proper drainage systems, heavy rain accumulates much more readily on pavement than on soil. The scenes are repeated over and over—for example, in Dallas-Fort Worth and Kansas City earlier this year. The sky opens up and roads become torrents.

ARE THERE MORE HURRICANES? NO.

The number of U.S. land-falling major hurricanes (maximum sustained winds over 110 mph) has gone down: 23 from 1940–69 and only 14 since 1970. However, damage caused by hurricanes and other powerful ocean storms has increased markedly since the '40s. Taking inflation into account, hurricane damage costs went up from $36.8 billion from the years 1940–69 to nearly $74.9 billion from 1970–96. So what's the deal? Again ponder the explosion of increasingly more expensive coastal development. With nearly uninhibited growth continuing along the nation's coasts and the inevitability of strong ocean storms, losses will continue to rise.

ARE THERE MORE TORNADOES? MAYBE.

The number of *reported* tornadoes in the United States has more than doubled from the '50s to the '90s. "Reported," however, is misleading; the actual number of tornadoes has not necessarily risen during that time. If a tornado occurred and no one was around to see it or document its damage path, then for the purpose of official numbers, it truly did not occur. Even today, there is evidence suggesting that many tornadoes go undetected.

There are good explanations as to why reported tornado numbers have risen so dramatically. Simply put, there are more people to witness tornadoes. Then consider the X factor: storm chasers. Virtually non-existent in the '50s, there are now hundreds who tote palm-held camcorders into the Plains to tape the Big One. It only makes sense the numbers of reported tornadoes are way up.

In the last few years, tornado-related deaths in America have risen. That's because a few tornadoes have hit densely populated communities. Of the more than 1,400 reported tornadoes and 130 tornado-related deaths in 1998, four twisters were responsible for 82 of the fatalities. Bottom line: Tornadoes can be frighteningly fierce and although the probability that one will hit a densely populated region is small, it can and does happen.

When taking a peek at the more distant past Richard Alley from Penn State University discovered through ice-core measurements that global temperatures and precipitation in the last few thousand years have been as steady as any time during the last 100 millennia. He also found that large swings in temperature (15 degrees Fahrenheit) and wet weather occurred on a regular basis prior to the recent quieter time. Perhaps more interesting is that these swings, which happened long before humans had a chance to influence the environment, typically occurred within a 10-year period, indicating that drastic climate change can occur through natural means, and quickly.

This evidence raises an interesting and provocative idea. Perhaps wilder weather is actually more typical than benign weather.

Whether humans are contributing to climate change or not, maybe the pendulum is beginning to swing back—toward the wild side. ∾

The Last Street

ABRAHAM REISEN

TRANSLATED FROM THE YIDDISH BY LEONARD WOLF

The last street of the town;
And there the final house.
The place seems like a joke
After the city's noise.

The neighbors are so hushed,
Each house so small—
Which makes the fields seem broad,
The sky especially full.

And everywhere you look
Your eyes with pleasure shine.
Here where the city ends,
The world begins.

RESPONDING TO CLUSTER FOUR

Thinking Skill SYNTHESIZING

1. Each of the other clusters in this book is introduced by a question that is meant to help readers focus their thinking about the selections. What do you think the question for Cluster Four should be?

2. How do you think the selections in this cluster should be taught? Demonstrate your ideas by joining with your classmates to

   ◆ create discussion questions.

   ◆ lead discussions about the selections.

   ◆ develop vocabulary activities.

   ◆ prepare a cluster quiz.

REFLECTING ON *WHAT ON EARTH?*

Essential Question HOW DO WE PROTECT OUR PLANET?

Reflecting on this book as a whole provides an opportunity for independent learning and the application of the critical thinking skill, synthesis. *Synthesizing* means examining all the things you have learned from this book and combining them to form a richer and more meaningful view of how we protect the earth.

There are many ways to demonstrate what you know about protecting the earth. Here are some possibilities. Your teacher may provide others.

1. Individually or with a small group, research one of the topics that was covered in this book: weather patterns, wildlife in the suburbs, hunting, animal research, or the Exxon Valdez oil spill in Prince Edward Sound. Present your information in a speech, essay, or debate. Then explain whether you think the authors of the selections in this book presented their information in fair or biased ways.

2. Create an environmental report card for your town, grading it in categories that you think are important, such as general awareness of ecological issues, recycling, and so on. Then gather information by interviewing city officials or longtime residents on how things have changed in the last ten years. What's better? What's worse?

3. Develop a video, report, or photo essay on an environmental problem in your school or community. Then develop a plan of action to address the problem.

AUTHOR BIOGRAPHIES

HARVEY ARDEN For twenty-three years, Harvey Arden worked as a staff writer at *National Geographic* magazine. He has also written and edited several books about indigenous people in the United States. Arden has retired from *National Geographic,* but he continues to work on novels, plays, screenplays, and nonfiction books. Arden is coauthor, with Steven Wall, of the best-selling book *Wisdomkeepers: Meetings with Native American Spiritual Elders.*

DAVE BARRY Born in New York in 1947, Dave Barry notes in his online biography that he "has been steadily growing older ever since without ever actually reaching maturity." A natural comedian, Barry's writing career began with short humor pieces that he wrote for his high school newspaper. He was an English major in college and has worked as a writer his entire life. From 1983 to 2005, Barry wrote commentary for the *Miami Herald.* Barry has written 23 books and won numerous awards, including the Pulitzer Prize for commentary in 1988. His nonliterary endeavors have included the CBS sitcom "Dave's World," based on two of his books, and playing lead guitar in the rock band Rock Bottom Remainders, made up entirely of authors— including Stephen King and Amy Tan. Barry lives with his wife and children in Miami, Florida.

RAY BRADBURY Born in 1920 in Waukegan, Illinois, Ray Bradbury once described the act of writing as "a fever—something I must do. And it seems I always have some new fever developing, some new love to follow and bring to life." As if to back up that claim, he wrote his first story at age eleven on butcher paper. Since then, Bradbury has published more than 500 short stories, novels, plays, screenplays, television scripts, and poems. Many, such as *The Martian Chronicles, The Illustrated Man, Fahrenheit 451,* and *Something Wicked This Way Comes,* have been best sellers. All have been wildly creative, blending contemporary issues with fantastical science fiction to make observations about the way we live today. Among his many awards are the O. Henry Memorial Award, the Benjamin Franklin Award, the World Fantasy Award for Lifetime Achievement, and the Grand Master Award from the Science Fiction Writers of America. He received the National Book Foundation Medal for his distinguished contribution to American letters.

ANTHONY BRANDT is a book columnist for *National Geographic Adventure* magazine and a writer who publishes his own nonfiction in major magazines such as *The New York Times* and *The Atlantic Monthly.* He recently spent an entire year editing the journals of Lewis and Clark for publication.

WILLIAM J. BROOKE Born in 1946, William J. Brooke has become well known for his fantasy writing for young adults. His tall tales, imaginative fiction, and creative nonfiction are all very popular with readers of all ages. Among his most popular books are *Teller of Tales,* a collection of six retold fairy tales, and *A Brush with Magic,* based on a Chinese tale about a boy whose magic brush paints images that come to life.

JOSEPH BRUCHAC His ethnic heritage includes American Indian, Slovak, and English ancestors, but Joseph Bruchac identifies most strongly with his Abenaki lineage. He brings the gifts of that heritage to his writing, teaching, and storytelling. Working from a rich oral tradition, Bruchac develops broad, memorable characters who teach as well as entertain. He has presented these characters and their stories at storytelling venues throughout Europe and the United States. Bruchac has won many awards, including the Cherokee Nation Prose Award, the Knickerbocker Award, and the Hope S. Dean Award for Notable Achievement in Children's Literature. In 1999, he won the Lifetime Achievement Award from the Native Writers Circle of the Americas. In addition to writing and telling stories, Bruchac is dedicated to preserving Abenaki culture and language, including traditional and contemporary Abenaki music.

RACHEL CARSON Born in 1907 on a farm in Pennsylvania, Rachel Carson was first introduced to the natural environment by her mother. She later became a writer for a radio show, "Romance Under the Waters," in which she brought to listeners the fascinating life of undersea creatures. After earning an MA in zoology from Johns Hopkins University, she took a job with the U.S. Bureau of Fisheries, where she worked until 1952, becoming chief editor of all publications for the U.S. Fish and Wildlife Service. She wrote several articles about the beauty of nature before embarking on *Silent Spring,* a potent argument against the use of poisonous chemicals in the environment. Chemical industry professionals and their political supporters attacked Carson's book, but it was well researched and it influenced President John F. Kennedy to call for testing of the chemicals mentioned in the book. Carson died of breast cancer in 1964.

JOHN CIARDI John Ciardi was born in 1916 and became one of the 20th century's most well-respected poets. He wrote award-winning poems for children as well as adults and has been called the world's best English-language translator of Dante. In addition to working as a professor of English, Ciardi served as poetry editor for *Saturday Review* and director of the Bread Loaf Writers' Conference. Ciardi once said, "You don't have to suffer to be a poet; adolescence is enough suffering for anyone." He died in 1986.

SEVERN CULLIS-SUZUKI At the age of twelve, Severn Cullis-Suzuki and her friends founded a group called ECO to raise money for environmental causes. The group held bake sales and fundraisers to pay its way to a worldwide environmental summit in Rio De Janeiro, Brazil, where Cullis-Suzuki gave a speech to those assembled. Over the next several years, Cullis-Suzuki earned a degree in ecology and evolutionary biology from Yale. Today, she works as an environmental activist.

GREGG EASTERBROOK was born in Buffalo, New York, to Canadian parents who moved to the United States. He works as a senior editor at *The New Republic* and is a contributing editor for *The Atlantic Monthly* and *The Washington Monthly*. Easterbrook is a visiting fellow at the Brookings Institution. His latest book is *The Progress Paradox: How Life Gets Better While People Feel Worse*.

PHILIP JOSÉ FARMER is a fantasy and science fiction writer who has written more than 70 books and 100 short stories. He has won three Hugo Awards, a Grand Master Award, and the World Fantasy Award for Lifetime Achievement. Farmer was born in North Terre Haute, Indiana, and lives in Peoria, Illinois. You can read more about Farmer on his Web page: < www.pjfarmer.com > .

ANDREW HOLLEMAN When he was a twelve-year-old amateur naturalist, the woods that Andrew Holleman loved were threatened by a developer. Holleman's research and activism saved the parcel of land from unwise development. When asked five years later what advice he would give other young people with a dream, Holleman replied, "You can never give up the fight; if you believe in something you have to stand up for it, and that's just the way it is."

H. M. HOOVER Her parents instilled in H. M. Hoover a love of books and a deep respect for nature. After college, Hoover tried several jobs but was not happy with any of them. She then decided to give herself four years in which to establish a career as a writer. Four years later, she published her first children's science fiction novel, *Children of Morrow,* and began the career that has lasted more than twenty years. Hoover has published over fifteen novels to date.

JOE KANE A successful journalist who has participated in several expeditions through South America, Joe Kane has documented the struggles of indigenous people who face economic and cultural colonization by rich corporations. When he is not traveling the world, Kane lives in the state of Washington with his wife and two children.

COLIN MARQUIS and **STU OSTRO** Colin Marquis is the senior director of weather communications at < www.weather.com >. He has also written for < www.usaweekend.com >. Colin Marquis is senior meteorologist at the Weather Channel. He also writes for the magazine *Weatherwise*. Marquis and Ostro have worked together as meteorologists for the Weather Channel. They write and speak often about weather-related issues.

JIM WAYNE MILLER In addition to being a poet, Jim Wayne Miller was a novelist, essayist, teacher, editor, and translator of books written in German. Born in North Carolina in 1936 and raised with five younger siblings on a farm in Kentucky, Miller was dedicated to writing and promoting Appalachian literature. Though he won many awards for his writing, some say his true legacy lies in the many writers he mentored and influenced, such as Emil Lerperger, Jesse Stuart, Cratis Williams, and James Still. Miller died in 1996.

MARY OLIVER Born in 1935 in Cleveland, Ohio, Mary Oliver now lives in Provincetown, Massachusetts. She attended Ohio State University for one year and then transferred to Vassar, at the time a women's college. Her poetry is influenced by the poetry of Edna St. Vincent Millay. In 1984, her poetry collection *American Primitive* won the Pulitzer Prize. In 1986, she moved to Bucknell University where she was honored with the title "poet in residence." In 1991, she moved to Sweet Briar College in Virginia. Her poetry, which grows out of her appreciation for nature, continues to win numerous awards.

KATHERINE PATERSON When Katherine Paterson was ten, she wanted to be either a movie star or a missionary. When she was twenty, she wanted to get married and have lots of children. But after her church hired her to write some educational materials, she became a writer. Paterson confesses that she sometimes thinks she will never have another good idea. Then a character crosses her imagination and she writes a new novel. She feels lucky to be living a writer's life.

GARY PAULSEN At the age of fourteen, Gary Paulsen ran away from an unhappy home and joined the circus. His taste for adventure led him to work as a farmhand, engineer, construction worker, truck driver, rancher, sailor, and dog trainer for the Iditarod, an Alaskan dogsled race. Some of these life experiences are reflected in the more than 175 books he has written for children and young adults. His novels *Hatchet, Dogsong,* and *The Winter Room* are all Newbery Honor books. What keeps the author at his desk for up to twenty hours a day? As one biographer put it, "It is Paulsen's overwhelming belief in young people that drives him to write."

DAVID QUAMMEN Growing up with aspirations to be a writer, David Quammen published his first book while still a student at Yale. After attending graduate school at Oxford, he moved to Bozemen, Montana, where he supported himself by waiting tables and bartending while devoting himself to writing. He wrote for *Outside* magazine from 1981 to 1995 and won the National Magazine Award twice. Quammen writes primarily about his adopted state of Montana, where he continues to live and work.

ABRAHAM REISEN Born in Minsk in 1876, Abraham Reisen moved to the United States when he was an adult. Reisen was a prolific poet and writer, often writing stories about the travails of Jewish people for the Yiddish daily papers. He became a valued recorder of his times whose work is still studied today. Reisen died in 1953.

BARBARA RUSH is a writer and reteller of folktales and the author of several nonfiction books about Jewish tradition, including *The Jewish Year: Celebrating the Holidays* and *The Lights of Hanukkah*.

HOWARD SCHWARTZ A teacher, poet, and Jewish folklorist, Howard Schwartz describes his politics as "pro-human." He writes and edits both children's books and books for adults, and his work has won numerous awards. Currently, Schwartz works as a professor of English at the University of Missouri at St. Louis.

GARY SOTO Born and raised in California, Gary Soto still makes his home there. In addition to his work for children, Soto has written ten poetry collections for adults, and his poems have won several prizes. He has also written for television and opera. Soto has received the Literature Award from the Hispanic Heritage Foundation, the Author-Illustrator Civil Rights Award from the National Education Association, and the PEN Center West Book Award for *Petty Crimes*. He also serves as Young People's Ambassador for the California Rural Legal Assistance (CRLA) and the United Farm Workers of America (UFW).

JESSICA SZYMCZYK works in a research laboratory. Her article on her experience as an animal lover in a biomedical lab, which appeared in *Newsweek* magazine, inspired serious dialogue in the magazine's letters section.

DAVID WAGONER Poet and novelist David Wagoner has written more than a dozen books of poetry, ten novels, and a study of Theodore Roethke's work. Wagoner has won several prizes and fellowships; his *Collected Poems* was nominated for the National Book Award. He was the editor of *Poetry Northwest* and a chancellor of the American Academy of Poets. Currently he lives and writes in the state of Washington.

STEVE WALL An oral and visual historian, Steve Wall has traveled to every state and more than 40 different countries. He has worked on stories for the National Geographic Society and United Press International, and his photos have been exhibited around the world. During the past twenty years, he has worked with Native American and indigenous spiritual elders throughout the Americas. He is the photographer and coauthor with Harvey Arden of the best-selling *Travels in a Stone Canoe: The Return to the Wisdomkeepers*. He is also the author and photographer of four other books.

ADDITIONAL READING

Ecology, Steve Pollock. Eyewitness Science. ©1992

Hoot, Carl Hiaasen. Roy, who is new to his small Florida community, becomes involved in another boy's attempt to save a colony of burrowing owls from a proposed construction site. Newbery Honor. ©2002

Lostman's River, Cynthia DeFelice. Ty MacCauley comes to grips with his disturbing discovery that good and evil are not absolutes, and at the same time his parents must decide whether they will keep hiding or face the future. ©1995

The Missing 'Gator of Gumbo Limbo, Jean Craighead George. Liza, one of five homeless people living in an unspoiled forest in southern Florida, searches for a missing alligator destined for official extermination and studies the delicate ecological balance keeping her outdoor home beautiful. ©1993

Pilgrim at Tinker Creek, Annie Dillard. A personal narrative on ecology and the importance of nature from the author's one-year exploration of her own neighborhood. Pulitzer Prize winner. ©1998

A Place Called Ugly, Avi. At the end of the summer, fourteen-year-old Owen refuses to leave the beach house which has been his family's summer home for ten years and is scheduled for demolition. ©1995

Shadowmaker, Joan Lowery Nixon. After she and her mother move to a small Texas town and experience a series of menacing events, Katie begins to suspect there is something sinister going on involving a secret gang of high schoolers and illegally stored toxic waste. ©1995

Shadows in the Water, Kathryn Lasky. When Mr. Starbuck accepts a job with the Environmental Protection Agency, the family moves to a houseboat in the Florida Keys. They soon discover the fragile ecosystem of the Keys is in danger and set out to stop the culprits. ©1992

The Talking Earth, Jean Craighead George. Billie Wind ventures out alone into the Florida Everglades to test the legend of her Indian ancestors and learns the importance of listening to the earth's vital messages. ©1987

The Weirdo, Theodore Taylor. In this environmental thriller, seventeen-year-old Chip Clewt fights to save the black bears in the Powhatan National Wildlife Refuge. ©1993

Who Really Killed Cock Robin? An Ecological Mystery, Jean Craighead George. A compelling ecological mystery that provides a timely and important message, explaining why nature must be kept in balance and how the actions of people affect life everywhere. ©1992

The Wolfling, Sterling North. In the 19th-century Midwest, a young boy adopts a wolf whelp and gains the attention and friendship of the Swedish American naturalist Thure Kumlien. ©1992

Acknowledgments

CONTINUED FROM PAGE 2

"The Growin' of Paul Bunyan" by William J. Brooke. Text copyright © 1990 by William J. Brooke. Used by permission of HarperCollins Publishers.

"Is Humanity a Special Threat?" from *A Moment on the Earth* by Gregg Easterbrook, copyright © 1995 by Gregg Easterbrook. Used by permission of Viking Penguin, a division of Penguin Putnam Inc.

"The King of the Beasts" published by permission of Philip José Farmer c/o Ralph M. Vicinanza, Ltd.

"The Last Dog" copyright © 1999 by Katherine Paterson. Reprinted from *Tomorrowland: Stories about the Future,* by permission of Scholastic, Inc.

"The Mushroom" by Helen M. Hoover. Copyright H. M. Hoover.

"Nacho Loco" from *Local News*, copyright © 1993 by Gary Soto, reprinted by permission of Harcourt, Inc.

"Only a Little Planet" by Lawrence Collins. Reprinted by permission of Friends of the Earth.

"A Palace of Bird Beaks" copyright © 1991 by Howard Schwartz and Barbara Rush. Used by permission of HarperCollins Publishers.

"A Sound of Thunder" by Ray Bradbury. Reprinted by permission of Don Congdon Associates, Inc. Copyright © 1952 by Crowell-Collier Publishing, renewed 1980 by Ray Bradbury.

"The Sun" by Mary Oliver. From *New and Selected Poems* by Mary Oliver. Copyright © 1992 by Mary Oliver. Reprinted by permission of Beacon Press, Boston.

"When Nature Comes Too Close" by Anthony Brandt. Reprinted with permission from the August 1998 *Reader's Digest* and Anthony Brandt. Originally appeared in *Audubon* in 1997.

"Wisdomkeepers" by Harvey Arden and Steve Wall. Used by permission of Beyond Words Publishing.

"Working against Time" by David Wagoner. From *Traveling Light*. Copyright 1999 by David Wagoner. Used with permission of the poet and the University of Illinois Press.

"A Young Environmentalist Speaks Out" by Severn Cullis-Suzuki, from a speech in Brazil, 1992. Reprinted by permission of the author.

Every reasonable effort has been made to properly acknowledge ownership of all material used. Any omissions or mistakes are not intentional and, if brought to the publisher's attention, will be corrected in future editions.